A Teacher's Manual on
Visions and Dreams

By
Mary J. Ogenaarekhua

A Teacher's Manual on
Visions and Dreams

Endorsements

"As one who has been involved in the development of Mary's prophetic ministry and leadership skills, it is evident that she has utilized her gifting to bring a balance of the spiritual and the practical aspects of interpreting dreams and visions. In **"A Teacher's Manual on Visions and Dreams,"** *Mary applies the same principles of prophetic activation to interpreting and activating dreams and visions. Through the unique insights of this manual, I believe God will use it as another way to bring revelation to His people."*

-Prophet David Jobson
Teacher-- Life Center Ministries,
Dunwoody, Georgia.

"We have been blessed to know and learn from the ministry gift known as Mary Ogenaarekhua. "Mary O." flows in her God-given anointing and is eager to share with others. Secure Foundation Bible Church, where we pastor, declares that its mission is to inform, activate and empower. Mary Ogenaarekhua does exactly that by removing the veil of misinformation and secrecy. She informs us through the Word of God, activates us through the workshop application and empowers us through the impartation of the Anointing of the Holy Ghost. We encourage pastors and leaders to avail themselves of this wonderful opportunity."

-Pastors David and Joyce Smith
Secure Foundation Bible Church, Georgia.

*"**A Teacher's Manual on Visions and Dreams** is an invaluable armamentarium in the arsenal of any believer wanting to better understand and decode the source and meaning of spiritual messages revealed during the depth of sleep. As a physician trained and used to dealing with the physical sciences, attending Mary's workshops has helped open my scientific mind to the reality of the spiritual realm."*

-Jonathan Nwiloh, MD

A Teacher's Manual on Visions and Dreams

All scriptures are quoted from the King James and the New King James versions of the Bible.

Published by To His Glory Publishing Company, Inc.®
111 Sunnydale Court
Lawrenceville, GA 30044
(770) 458-7947
www.tohisglorypublishing.com
www.maryjministries.com

Book is available at:
Amazon.com, BarnesandNoble.com, Borders.com, etc.
This book can also be special ordered through any of your local bookstores.
www.tohisglorypublishing.com

Cover designed by: Obasi Scott, Shepherds Loft LLC.

International Standard Book Number: 0-9749802-0-X

Foreword

Dreams--Some are happy and some are sad. Some are comforting and some are disturbing. Some are scary and some are just downright funny. (Many times at night, I have awakened myself laughing out loud.)

Some dreams are remembered and some are forgotten. Some dreams are natural and others are spiritual.

No matter what kind of dreams you have, one thing is certain: You do dream! God created us with the ability and need to both sleep and dream.

The Bible records God prophetically speaking to individuals in dreams. Joseph of the Old Testament was a dreamer and interpreter of dreams. He changed the course of nations through the gift of interpretation of dreams when he interpreted Pharaoh's dream.

The Joseph in the New Testament received the name Jesus for Mary's son in a spiritual or prophetic dream. This name, Jesus, has the ability to shake nations and pull down kingdoms. There is power in the name of Jesus. I remind you again--this precious name was given to Joseph in a dream.

God is still speaking to mankind in dreams today. More of God's people are beginning to recognize their spiritual dreams from their natural dreams and in doing so, the obvious question arises, "How do I know what the dream means?"

In interpreting dreams, one cannot adopt the mind-set that certain symbols have to always represent the same things. God meant for us to depend on the Holy Spirit for spiritual interpretation of our dreams. God is showing His people more and more about activating our spiritual gifts, and He is provoking reaction to His Voice through visions and dreams. Hallelujah!

Mary Ogenaarekhua (affectionately known to Life Center family and friends as Mary O.) learned as a child that God is a powerful and purposeful giver of life. At the age of eight years, Mary O. was pronounced dead when she took a fatal fall.

The Muslim officials in the Nigerian town where she lived with her grandparents would not allow her to be buried in the Muslim cemetery because of her Christian name–Justina. God was in control and, of course, as you know–He raised Mary from the dead! What a God! What a testimony! In 1994, the Lord gave her the name Mary, so she is now known as Mary Justina.

Mary loves God, respects His Truth, and is devoted to obeying and serving Him. This causes her to pull on all that courage that He has graced her with. She is fearless in her pursuit of God and in encouraging those around her to know and obey the Truth, as well as to live and practice that same truth.

One way God is speaking to individuals today is through visions and dreams. Christians have to

understand what God is saying to them to be able to obey Him.

Mary O.'s **A _Teacher's Manual on Visions and Dreams_** is a good source for starting to learn how to understand and interpret visions and dreams. It is a good foundation upon which to build.

-Dr. Mary Crum
Life Center Ministries
Dunwoody, Georgia

Dedication

I dedicate this manual to God the Father, God the Son and God the Holy Ghost. Lord Jesus, You said to me, "Go and get yourself baptized and I will show you things." You have kept Your promise to me. Truly, all good gifts and all perfect gifts come from You, O God, and of your own do we give unto You. You are worthy. I pray that you will use this manual to teach your teachers about visions and dreams.

I also dedicate this manual to Apostle Buddy Crum and Prophet Mary Crum--Senior Pastors at Life Center Ministries, Dunwoody, Georgia. Prophet Mary, God has used you to set up a modern day school of the prophets where many come to be trained, equipped and released to do the work of the Lord. I heard one thing from you that has opened a whole new horizon for me in the prophetic realm—ACTIVATION! Thank you for teaching and activating me to use my God-given gifts. Thank you also for my other Life Center teachers that were trained by you. You are truly a teacher's teacher.

This manual is also dedicated to the students in the Visions and Dream Class. I thank you all for being great students. You are always eager to learn new truths from the Word of God. I love you all. Thank you, Robin, Anita, Janis, and Misa for your willingness to share your interpretations of the dreams addressed in this manual.

Table of Contents

Preface

Because Christians and non-Christians dream, this manual is designed to help anyone desiring knowledge about visions and dreams. However, since it is the Holy Spirit that actually interprets visions and dreams, an individual would need to have a personal revelation of the saving grace of the Lord Jesus Christ before he or she could operate the gift of interpreting visions and dreams God's way, or understand visions and dreams more accurately.

This is a teacher's outline of the basic principles that any student in a visions and dreams class must master in order to operate the gift of seeing effectively. The manual is not designed to restrict or confine the God-given gift of seeing, but rather to enhance it and give the student proper instruction. This is a teacher's aid that is meant to facilitate classroom discussions and dialogues to help students or church members understand more accurately how, and why, God uses visions and dreams.

This manual is also designed to help pastors, teachers, book clubs and Bible study groups conduct classes on visions and dreams. The format has been simplified to make this an easy task. It is designed to instruct those who would be called upon to teach others skills and understanding in visions and in dreams.

The recommended textbook for students in this class is *Keys to Understanding Your Visions and Dreams: A Classroom Approach.* It is also available at Amazon.com, BarnesandNoble.com, booksamillion.com, tohisglorypublishing.com etc.

Note: *The names of some of the individuals in this manual have been changed to protect their identity. Any coincidence with the real name of any one in the general public is not intentional.*

Mary J. Ogenaarekhua

Acknowledgements

Thank you, Robin Bright. You are a true trooper in the Lord. Your question to me, "Mary, how come you do not have your notes typed?" resulted in this manual. May God greatly reward you for your seeds of time and effort that you have planted into the work of my ministry. Thanks for all your behind-the-scenes work on this project. And you can barbeque, girl!!! I love you, sister.

Pastor Chris Oyakhilome--Christ Embassy, Nigeria. You led me to the Lord in 1992 and you were also the first person I heard preach on visions and dreams. Thank you. Pastor Anita, I love you.

Pastor Bridget Ogbah--Gospel Pavilion, Nigeria. See, your prayers for me were not in vain. Not only did I get saved, I actually live and work for the Lord now! I love you, Pastor Theo.

Thank you, Pastor Samuel Rose and Pastor Laura Lee Rose--Associate Pastors at Life Center Ministries. Pastor Sam, I stand amazed, always, at the sincere love from a pure heart that God has given you. Pastor Laura Lee, thank you for releasing me to teach the class on visions and dreams. This manual and the accompanying textbook are the direct result of that release. You, too, are a great blessing to many others as well as to me.

Thank you, Elders Patricia Fraley, David Jobson and Catherine Sykes. You all were well trained by Prophet Mary Crum and, as a result, became the vessels that God used to also teach, equip and activate me in the prophetic realm. You are great teachers.

Thank you, Rupert and Leila Williams for your support and encouragement. I greatly appreciate your help in the business aspect of my ministry. Ms. Leila, it was you who insisted that I must "pass the baton" and teach others about visions and dreams. You stayed on me till I began a class on visions and dreams. Like a very determined mother, your insistence paid off. Thanks.

Thank you Jennye Guy for editing this book. I truly appreciate your help. God bless you.

Thank you Patrick Lantey for your work on the layout of this book. You did a great job!

Frequently Asked Questions

- Does God really speak to us in dreams?
- Does every dream have a meaning?
- Should dreams be ignored?
- What should you do when you have the same dream over and over?
- What does a particular color mean in a dream?
- What does it mean when you see your dead relative or friend in a dream?
- What does it mean when you see someone lying in a casket?
- What does it mean when you are being chased or pursued in a dream?
- What happens when you wake up from a dream and cannot remember it?
- Do we dream because we ate the wrong food or too much?
- How do you know whether a dream is God's warning or from the devil?
- How long do you seek an answer to the meaning of a dream?
- Should you ask for interpretations? Should you only seek interpretations from God?

You will find answers to these and many other questions as you read this manual and the accompanying textbook, *Keys to Understanding Your Visions and Dreams: A Classroom Approach.*

How to Conduct a Class

And the things that thou hast heard of me among many witnesses, the same commit thou to faithful men, who shall be able to teach others also-- 2 Timothy 2:2.

1. Use forty-five to fifty minutes to teach each lesson.
2. Use about ten to fifteen minutes to answer questions.
3. Use about ten minutes to activate the students by the laying on of hands. **(The initial laying on of hands should be done by someone who walks in the anointing of interpretation of visions and dreams.** Feel free to contact us at maryjministries.com for the initial activation class.)

4. Use one hour on interpretation of visions and dreams.

LESSON 1

Key Principles about Visions and Dreams

Basic Understanding: We must be very clear in our understanding of what God's plan and purposes are for our lives. It is His will that we know, see and apprehend with our spiritual eyes those things that He has for us. This means that our spiritual eyes of understanding must be enlightened as stated in Ephesians 1:18:

> The <u>eyes of your understanding being enlightened</u>; that ye may know what is the hope of his calling, and what the riches of the glory of his inheritance in the saints…

And in 1 Corinthians 2:9-12:

> But as it is written, Eye hath not seen, nor ear heard, neither have entered into the heart of man, the things which God hath prepared for them that love him. But God hath revealed them unto us by his Spirit: for the Spirit searcheth all things, yea, the deep things of God. For what man knoweth the things of a man, save the spirit of man which is in him? Even so the things of God knoweth no man, but the Spirit of God. Now we have received, not the spirit of the world, but the Spirit which is of God; <u>that we might know the things that are freely given to us of God.</u>

We must be able to bring into the physical realm those things that God shows us in the spiritual realm through visions and dreams. This is why God told Abraham in Gen 13:14-15:

> Lift up now thine eyes, and look from the place where thou art northward, and southward, and eastward, and westward: <u>For all the land which thou seest, to thee will I give it</u>, and to thy seed forever.

It is God's will that we succeed in His plans for us. Therefore, He gives us visions and dreams so that we can agree with Him. When we agree with Him, we can then with our faith bring those plans into the physical realm. The key word is "see."

Key: If you can see it, you can have it. You cannot have it if you cannot see it.

Motto: Those who cannot see the invisible cannot do the impossible.

The natural man is guided by his senses but the new creation is lead by the Holy Spirit. God promised the gifts of visions and dreams to all flesh. We see this in Joel 2:28:

> And it shall come to pass afterward, that I will pour out my spirit upon all flesh; and your sons and your daughters shall prophesy, your old men shall dream dreams, your young men shall see visions.

Also, in 2 Corinthians 5:7 we are told that we **walk by faith and not by sight.**

Reasons God Uses Visions and Dreams

God said in Numbers 12:6:

> **If there be a prophet among you, I, the Lord, will <u>make myself known unto him in a vision</u> and <u>speak to him in a dream</u>.**

From the above scripture, we see that God uses visions and dreams to:

1. Make Himself Known to Us

It is God's will that we know Him and that we are not in darkness, even in the knowledge of who He is. John 8:12 states:

> **Then spake Jesus again unto them, saying, I am the light of the world: he that followeth me shall not walk in darkness, but shall have the light of life.**

2. Speak to Us

God uses dreams to speak to us. God spoke to Joseph in dreams about his future. Joseph was very pleased with God's plans for him.

Review **<u>Dreams</u>** Genesis 37:5-11:

> And Joseph dreamed a dream, and he told it his brethren: and they hated him yet the more.
> And he said unto them, Hear, I pray you, this dream which I have dreamed:
> For, behold, we were binding sheaves in the field, and, lo, my sheaf arose, and also stood upright; and, behold, your sheaves stood round about, and made obeisance to my sheaf.
> And his brethren said to him, Shalt thou indeed reign over us? Or shalt thou indeed have dominion over us? And they hated him yet the more for his dreams, and for his words.
> And he dreamed yet another dream, and told it his brethren, and said, Behold, I have dreamed a dream more; and, behold, the sun and the moon and the eleven stars made obeisance to me.
> And he told it to his father, and to his brethren: and his father rebuked him, and said unto him, what is this dream that thou hast dreamed? Shall I and thy mother and thy brethren indeed come to bow down ourselves to thee to the earth?
> And his brethren envied him; but his father observed the saying.

3. Give Us Divine Promotion

God used dreams to supernaturally promote both Joseph **(Gen 41:41)** and Daniel **(Daniel 2:48).**

We see in the following scriptures how Pharaoh was very impressed by the Spirit that was in Joseph. Pharaoh said to Joseph in Gen 41:15:

I have heard say of thee, that thou canst understand a dream to interpret it.

And in Genesis 41:38-40:

Can we find such a one as this is, a man in whom the Spirit of God is? ... Forasmuch as God hath shewed thee all this, there is none so discreet and wise as thou art: Thou shall be over my house and according unto thy word shall all my people be ruled: only in the throne will I be greater than thou.

Study Daniel 2:28 and see how God used the interpretation of a dream to promote Daniel and his friends. The secret of the king's dream is revealed to Daniel **(Daniel 2:19.)**

But there is a God in heaven that revealeth secrets, and maketh known to the king Nebuchadnezzar what shall be in the latter days. Thy dream, and the visions of thy head upon thy bed, are these...

Nebuchadnezzar was very impressed by the Spirit that was in Daniel. In Daniel 5:12, **the** Queen said about Daniel:

For as much as an excellent spirit and knowledge and understanding, interpreting of dreams dissolving of doubts were found in the same Daniel.

And in Daniel 2:47 Nebuchadnezzar said:

Of a truth it is that your God is a God of gods and Lord of Kings and a revealer of secrets, seeing thou couldest reveal this secret.

- Nebuchadnezzar fell down to worship Daniel because Daniel was able to reveal and interpret his dream.

Note: In the privacy of your home, you can ask God to reveal secrets to you through visions and dreams just like Daniel and his friends did. But, you cannot demand a vision or a dream from Him as doing so may open you to a spirit of deception. However, during activation in prophetic classes, you can believe God for a vision because the teacher and the other students can judge the vision for accuracy.

Teacher-- be certain to discuss the above point in detail.

4. To Show Us What He Has Given Us

Deuteronomy 29:29 states:

> **The secret things belong to the Lord our God but the things that are revealed belong to us and to our children forever**

God uses visions and dreams to show us what He has given us. We see this in
I Corinthians. 2:12:

> **Now we have received, not the spirit of the world, but the Spirit which is of God; <u>that we might know the things that are freely given to us of God.</u>**

5. Give Us Instructions

God uses visions and dreams to give instructions. We see this in the following instructions given to the wise men in Matthew 2:12:

> **And being warned of God in a dream that they should not return to Herod, they departed into their own country another way**

And in Matthew 2:13:

> **When they were departed, the Angel of the Lord appeared to Joseph in a dream saying, arise and take the young child and his mother and flee into Egypt and be thou there until I bring thee word.**

In Matthew 2:19-20:

> **But when Herod was dead, behold, an angel of the Lord appeared in a dream to Joseph in Egypt, Saying, arise, and take the young child and his mother, and go into the land of Israel: for they are dead which sought the young child's life**

6. To Warn Us

God will always warn us in a vision or dream when there is an unforeseen danger or when the devil lays a snare for us. Dreams are God's major tools to reach the unbelievers who do not know Him or His Word. Through dreams He can warn them about any danger. God will also use visions and dreams to woo people to Himself by stirring them up to seek answers.

Interpretation of dreams helps to resolve confusion and dispel ignorance.

· *Discuss your personal experiences of how God used dreams and visions to dispel your own ignorance.*

End Teaching Here

Activation

This is the part of the class where you gather the students together and:

· You identify new members in the class who are Spirit-filled and would like to receive the Anointing of skills in visions and dreams
· You lay hands on them to receive the Anointing **(Again, the initial laying on of hands should be done by someone who walks in the Anointing of interpretation of visions and dreams.)**
· You pray for the entire class.

Session on Actual Dreams and Their Interpretations

This is the part of the class where class members share their dreams and everyone extends their faith to the Lord for an understanding of the vision or dream.

Note:

· All interpretations must be based on scriptures.
· Everyone in the class should be allowed to participate, even if their answers are wrong.
· Listen carefully to identify any error in each answer as they speak **(use the blank notes at the end of each lesson to record each student's interpretation).**
· Allow everyone to give his or her interpretation before you address each response.
· Identify the inaccurate interpretations and address them.
· Summarize the accurate points that were identified by the students and address any portion of the dream still needing interpretation.

Note: Most students will skip portions of the dream that they do not understand, so be sure to address those portions.

Below is an actual dream. Examine the different interpretations and see what other revelations you and the students receive concerning it.

The Lumberyard Dream

A friend of mine had a dream that was located at her home church. There were members of the church standing around outside. Some were adults and some were children. She specifically remembered her husband, her father and herself being part of the group. In the natural, she remembers that the last time she was at the church, there was a lot of construction being done on the street. The church's property was being used to store lumber and the trucks and construction workers were going in and out of the property. This scene was also in the dream. She then noticed an SUV being driven by an unidentified Caucasian female. The driver was approaching the property and headed for the area where all of the lumber was gathered. In the natural, drivers often use the property in order to turn around. But the woman did not turn around; in fact, she seemed to accelerate in speed as she headed in the direction of the pile. She did not hit the lumber but collided into the trees. The front end of the car folded and the car exploded. She could see the face of the woman and that her head was crushed and bloody. Her father started running toward the scene to help. She was trying to rush the children away to safety so that they would not see. Everyone was in a state of pandemonium except her husband. He seemed completely oblivious to the fact that anything had happened and continued doing whatever he was doing. When she awoke, her heart was racing and she was struck that her husband had seemed completely unfazed as if he was unaware.

Interpretations

Note: Mary examines the interpretations given by the students and makes comments. Her comments to each student are in **boldface.** The *italicized words* are the student's words that Mary addressed

Misa's Interpretation

The vehicle may be an impending attack on the church, but the enemy will self-destruct. Your friend's husband must possess a peace that passes understanding.
Instructor: Misa, your first sentence is very good but you need to re-examine the one about the husband. In this dream, the husband is not discerning what is going on. It is not peace. It is either ignorance or spiritual slumber.

Anita's Interpretation

The church seems to be used as a place for "whatever" comes along. There is no respect for God's house and His property; it is not being reverenced as a house of corporate worship where we meet with God. The activities going on outside represent what is also going on inside naturally and spiritually with people; they have made a holy place--the church--and their personal relationship with the Lord as a common thing with no reverence. **Instructor: Anita, this is very good**.

The unidentified person is representing the enemy with his plan for destruction but the people don't recognize him because of their lukewarmness. They are watching him coming but are not seeing, so, when the enemy tried to attack (the unexpected happened) they were shaken in

disarray and confusion. **Instructor: Good.**

The way that they were trying to get the children to safety seems right, but it represents how they have covered their eyes from truth and the devil's tactics. **Instructor: It is more like they could not discern their spiritual state until there was danger (car crash).**

The tree that was ran into, that stopped the enemy, is the people who are planted by the streams of water that enabled them to crush Satan's head. **Instructor: Good**.

The husband seems to be oblivious to everything but he is representing those who are not moved or shaken--those who keep their focus, standing firm, grounded, and aware of Satan's devices. **Instructor: Anita, the opposite is the case here. The husband is not able to discern.**

It seems to say that the church needs to return to their First Love.

Robin's Interpretation

Gathering of the members outside the Church: Oh, how good and pleasant it is for brethren to dwell together in the house of the LORD!

Construction on the street: (Nehemiah's rebuilding of the walls)
God is in the process of bringing restoration that is not yet completed.

Church property used as storage (lumber, trucks, etc.): The material GOD intended to use can only be gathered from His Church.

Caucasian Woman in SUV: Those things that seem common are tools used by the enemy to bring catastrophe.

Husband (represents authority, protector): Those in authority are not aware of the destruction around them and continue business as usual.

Daughter, I have gathered a remnant together to watch the restoration process take place, but they are unaware of the planned dangers targeted to destroy those things I intended to use to bring wholeness, because those in authority have not discerned the pending dangers of the enemy for my church.

Instructor: Robin, this gathering and the state of this church are not to be exhorted. The church is nothing but a lumberyard. It is a place without spiritual discernment. The work they are doing is not godly. Your last sentence is good. You addressed the state of the church.

Mary's Comments

This dream is not good. It is not good for the church that is being addressed. Spiritually, it is a place where the members are just standing around. They are not involved in what God is doing. It is a place where those who are building are building with "hay, wood and stubble." It is a place that turns God's people around and away from the true work of God. In God's sight, it is nothing but a lumberyard! This is not good.

A few years ago, the Lord actually showed me a big church in, Georgia, where the Pastor was also filling up his lumberyard with more logs of wood. The Lord called his work hay, wood and stubble.

The children represent the believers under her care. She has a real concern for the children in the house of the Lord.

I forgot the part of the dream that stated that the husband was "oblivious" to what was going on around him. This means that he is not able to discern the spiritual environment around him or that he could care less. This will definitely play out in the type of work that he is doing.

The wife needs to pray that his spiritual eyes of understanding will be enlightened. The lady who was crushed was also familiar with hay,wood and stubble work; hence,she headed straight for the lumberyard. It was a good thing that her car (which represents the enemy) crashed.

Teacher's Notes and Students' Comments

Teacher's Notes and Students' Comments

Teacher's Notes and Students' Comments

Teacher's Notes and Students' Comments

LESSON 2

Sources of Your Visions and Dreams

1. God

The first source of your visions and dreams is God as stated in:

Joel 2:28:

> A. And it shall come to pass afterwards, that **I will pour out my Spirit upon all flesh**, and your sons and your daughters shall prophesy, **your old men shall dream dreams your young men shall see visions**.

Hosea 12:10:

> I have also spoken by the prophets, and **I have multiplied visions** and used similitudes, by the ministry of the prophets.

Psalm 32:8:

> I will instruct you and teach thee in way which thou shall go: I will guide thee with **mine eye**

* **Mine eye** speaks of the gift of seeing (visions and dreams)*

This is why the Old Testament Prophets were called **Seers** (Example: 1 Samuel 9:9). God uses prophets through dreams and visions to lead His people.

Job 33:14-18:

> For God speaketh once, yea twice, yet man perceiveth it not. **In a dream, in a vision of the night,** when deep sleep falleth upon men, in slumberings upon the bed; **Then he openeth the ears of men, and sealeth their instruction,** that He may withdraw man from his purpose, and hide pride from man. **He keepeth back his soul from the pit, and his life from perishing by the sword.**

Examples of Dreams from God

- **Genesis 41:25; 28**-- God shows Pharaoh what he is about to do
- **Daniel 2:28**-- God answers Nebuchadnezzar's heart's desire to know what would happen at the end time
- **Genesis 37:5--10** Joseph's dreams
- **Rev 1:1, Rev 1:10-11**-- Book of Revelation is about John's visions of end time events
- **Matthew 1:20**-- God spoke to Joseph instructing him to take Mary as his wife

Note: Visions and dreams are very important to God.

We see this in the following scriptures:

- · Amos 3:7: **Surely, the Lord will do nothing, but except He revealeth His secret to His servants the Prophets.**
- · Proverbs 29:18:
  Without a vision the people perish
- · Habakkuk 2:2:
  Write the vision and make it plain

2. The Devil

The second source of your visions and dreams is the devil, as he can also give you visions and dreams to deceive you. We cannot be ignorant of the devil's devices.

Note: Teacher, examine the following scripture to see what the Word says concerning the devil.

Concerning the devil, the Lord said in John 8:44:
He was a **murderer from the beginning** and **abode not in the truth**, because **there is no truth in him. When he speaketh a lie, he speaketh of his own: for he is a liar,** and **the father of it.**

Examples of the Devil's Lying Tactics

- • Matthew 13:24-30: **The parable of the tares** (the devil tries to sow tares of false visions and dreams while we sleep)
- • 2 Corinthians 11:14: **And no marvel; for Satan himself is transformed into an angel of light**
- • Genesis 3:4-7: He gave Eve false revelation (false visions) concerning the tree of the knowledge of good and evil
- • Matthew 4:8-9: **The devil showed the Lord all the kingdoms of this world and their glory**

Note: Teacher, let the students know that it possible for the devil to give someone a false vision and a false dream. Discuss in detail the temptation of the Lord Jesus and how the devil was able to show Him the kingdoms of this world and their glory.

Both God and the devil want your tongue, but only you can choose to whom you will yield it. The reason your tongue is in high demand is found in Proverbs 18:21:

Death and life are in the power of the tongue.

- • Do not let the devil use you as his mouthpiece to speak his evil plans that are shown through false dreams and visions. God is looking for those who will speak His words to establish His plans on earth. The devil is also looking for those who will help him speak his evil plans into existence. Cancel all evil visions and dreams.

3. Yourself

You are the third source of your visions and dreams. When you desire something greatly and begin to lust after it, you can get enticed and as a result, have false dreams and visions. An ungodly desire can deceive your heart as shown in James 1:14:

> **But every man is tempted, when he is drawn away of his own lust and enticed.**

Isaiah 29:7-8B:

> **Shall be as a dream or a night vision. It shall even be as when a hungry man dreameth, and behold, he eateth but; he awaketh, and his soul is empty; or as when a thirsty man dreameth, and behold, drinketh but when he awaketh, and behold, he is faint, and his soul hath appetite.**

Jeremiah 14:14:

> **Then the Lord said unto me, the prophets prophesy lies in my name: I sent them not, neither have I commanded them, neither spake unto them; they prophesy unto you a false vision and divination, and a thing of nought, and the deceit of their heart.**

Jeremiah 29:8C:

> **Neither hearken to your dreams which ye caused to be dreamed.**

Jeremiah 23:16:

> **They speak a vision of their own heart and not out of the mouth of the Lord.**

Jeremiah 23:26:

> **How long shall this be in the heart of the prophets that prophesy lies? Yea, they are prophets of the deceit of their own heart.**

End Teaching Here

Activation

Again, this is the part of the class where you gather the students together and:

- You identify new members in the class who are Spirit-filled and would like to receive the Anointing of skills in visions and dreams.
- You lay hands on them to receive the Anointing.
- You pray for the entire class.

Session on Actual Dreams and Their Interpretations

This is the part of the class where class members share their dreams and everyone extends their faith to the Lord for understanding of the vision or dream.

Note:

- All interpretations must be based on scriptures.
- Everyone in the class should be allowed to participate, even if their answers are wrong.
- Listen carefully to identify any error in each answer as the students speak (**use the blank notes at the end of each lesson to record each student's interpretation**).
- Allow everyone to give his or her interpretation before you address each response.
- Identify all inaccurate interpretations and address them.
- Summarize the accurate points that were identified by the students and address any portion of the dream still needing interpretation.

Note: Most students will skip portions of the dream that they do not understand, so be sure to address those portions of the dream.

Below is an actual dream. Examine the different interpretations and see what other revelations you and the students receive concerning it.

The Casket Dream

In my dream, I walked into the church of my former ministry and there was a funeral. It was the Pastor's husband in the casket; he is also the Bishop of her ministry. At this funeral there were a lot of people but only one of the Pastor's daughters attended. The Pastor has 10 children by her first husband and I was surprised in the dream that the rest of the family were not there for moral support. The daughter who was there acted as if his life didn't have any meaning. Before they closed the casket, she went up to the body and took off a necklace that was on the body and started having a discussion with another lady in the pulpit about the type of jewelry that she likes. The Pastor was sitting in her seat just looking sad, but she was not crying. Everyone one else seemed to be out of it. While all of this was going on, I was standing on the side of the pulpit feeling hurt that the Bishop was dead and saying to myself, "This can't be happening." The dream ended when I went toward the casket to tell the daughter, "Please don't bother this jewelry, it does not belong to you." I woke up before I could reach her.

Interpretations

Note: Mary examines the interpretations given by the students and makes comments. Her comments to each student are in **boldface.** The *italicized words* are the student's words that Mary addressed.

Anita's Interpretation

There is no respect for the husband (overseer). The wife's children seem to have been allowed to be disrespectful to authority because the wife ignored or failed to properly bring about discipline and honor by correction. This house is totally out of order and so it was in the church ministry; this is the state of both. **Instructor: Anita, this interpretation is right on.**

The bishop is like unto the Glory of God--the presence of the Holy Spirit that has gone. Eli allowed his children to have no reverence or honor for God and the place and people of authority: Icahabod. **Instructor: Yes, death <u>may</u> signify the departure of the spirit of God.**

Janis's Interpretation

I am receiving that this is about the "Church" in general and the state of the Body of Christ. This is through the eyes of the Father. We are His children, His Son (our husband/bridegroom) died for us and yet we still disregard Him and disrespect Him. We disregard authority and leaders. We take His gifts, His anointings and steal His glory. He is waiting for those that will come forward and take a stand for righteousness. Who will hear what the Spirit of the Lord is saying? **Instructor: The dream speaks of the pastor and her family. We must keep in mind that Jesus is risen from the dead. We cannot put Him in a casket. There is no resurrection in this dream so it cannot represent the Lord.**

Mary's Comments

This dream is to be canceled. The dead man in the casket is not the Lord because the Lord has risen from the dead; he is not in a casket!

The enemy is boasting of the things he is going to do to this man and his family. His plan is to kill the Pastor's husband and ruin the family relationship. We must proclaim that the plan shall not stand.

Pray that in the spirit and earth realms, this family would be a united family. Pray that greed, selfishness and the nonchalant attitude will not take root. Pray long life for the Pastor and do not share the dream with people anymore. This is a direct boast from the devil of what he is planning to do to this family. We cannot agree with it.

Teacher's Notes and Students' Comments

Teacher's Notes and Students' Comments

Teacher's Notes and Students' Comments

Teacher's Notes and Students' Comments

LESSON 3

How to Identify the Sources of Your Visions and Dreams

To effectively identify the sources of our visions and dreams, we need to know the truth about God the Father and God the Son and the truth about their ways. We need to be well-grounded in the knowledge of how they feel about us. They love us! Knowing the truth about them will help us to quickly identify when a vision or a dream misrepresents them.

In order to be able to detect a counterfeit, you must know the real very well.

Note: Teacher, use the example of how banks train their employees to detect counterfeit money by letting them handle large quantities of real money so that when they touch a counterfeit, it would feel strange to their hands.

The Truth about the Father and the Son

John 5:19-34 gives us a lot of information about God the Father, God the Son and God the Holy Spirit. It also tells us how they feel about us.

> Then answered Jesus and said unto them, Verily, verily, I say unto you, **The Son can do nothing of himself,** but **what he seeth the Father do: for what things soever he doeth, these also doeth the Son likewise.**
>
> For **the Father loveth the Son,** and **sheweth him all things that himself doeth:** and he will shew him greater works than these that ye may marvel.
>
> For as **the Father raiseth up the dead, and quickeneth them;** even so the son quickeneth whom he will.
>
> For **the Father judgeth no man,** but hath **committed all judgment unto the Son**
>
> That **all men should honour the Son, even as they honour the Father.**
>
> **He that honoureth not the Son honoureth not the Father** which hath sent him.
>
> Verily, verily, I say unto you, **He that heareth my word, and believeth on him that sent me, hath everlasting life, and shall not come into condemnation; but is passed from death unto life.**
>
> Verily, verily, I say unto you, The hour is coming, and now is, when **the dead shall hear the voice of the Son of God:** and **they that hear shall live.**
>
> For **as the Father hath life in himself; so hath he given to the Son to have life in himself;**
>
> And **hath given him authority to execute judgment** also, because he is the Son of man.
>
> Marvel not at this: for the hour is coming, in the which all that are in the graves shall hear his voice,
>
> And shall come forth; **they that have done good, unto the resurrection of life;** and they that have done evil, unto the resurrection of damnation.
>
> **I can of mine own self do nothing: as I hear, I judge:** and **my judgment is just;** because **I seek not mine own will, but the will of the Father which hath sent me.**
>
> **If I bear witness of myself, my witness is not true.**
>
> There is another that beareth witness of me; and I know that the witness which he

witnesseth of me is true.

Ye sent unto John, and he bare witness unto the truth.

But **I receive not testimony from man:** but **these things I say, that ye might be saved.**

From the above scripture, we see that:
- God loves us.
- God wants us to have life.
- God's judgments are just.
- Jesus is not bearing witness of Himself.
- Jesus does not seek His own will but the will of the Father
- Jesus is not presumptuous. He only does what He sees the Father do.
- He raises the dead.
- All who believe in Him and lead godly lives shall have eternal life.

Therefore, do not accept any vision or dream that does not line up with the above scripture. The next scriptures give us revelations of how God feels about us.

John 15:1-18: (Abiding in the Vine-Fruitfulness)

I am the true vine, and **my Father is the husbandman.**

Every branch in me that beareth not fruit he taketh away: and **every branch that beareth fruit, he purgeth it, that it may bring forth more fruit.**

Now **ye are clean through the word** which I have spoken unto you.

Abide in me, and I in you. As **the branch cannot bear fruit of itself,** except it abide in the vine; no more can ye, except ye abide in me.

I am the vine, ye are the branches: **He that abideth in me, and I in him, the same bringeth forth much fruit: for without me ye can do nothing.**

If a man abide not in me, he is cast forth as a branch, and is withered; and men gather them, and cast them into the fire, and they are burned.

If ye abide in me, and my words abide in you, ye shall ask what ye will, and it shall be done unto you.

Herein is my Father glorified, that ye bear much fruit; so shall ye be my disciples.

As the Father hath loved me, so have I loved you: continue ye in my love.

If ye keep my commandments, **ye shall abide in my love;** even as I have kept my Father's commandments, and abide in his love.

These things have I spoken unto you, **that my joy might remain in you,** and **that your joy might be full.**

This is my commandment, that ye love one another, as I have loved you.

Greater love hath no man than this, that a man lay down his life for his friends.

Ye are my friends, if ye do whatsoever I command you.

Henceforth I call you not servants; for the servant knoweth not what his lord doeth: but I have called you friends; **for all things that I have heard of my Father I have made known unto you.**

Ye have not chosen me, but I have chosen you, and ordained you, that ye should go and bring forth fruit, and that your fruit should remain: that whatsoever ye shall ask of the Father in my name, he may give it you.
These things I command you, that ye love one another.
If the world hate you, ye know that it hated me before it hated you.

Note: Teacher, be sure to point out to the students what the above scripture tells us about God the Father and the Lord Jesus. We know from this scripture that:
- Jesus is the true vine.
- We are the branches (we are connected to Him).
- The Father is the husbandman. He purges us to make us more fruitful and not to punish us.
- He wants us to bring forth much fruit.
- The Father is glorified when we bear much fruit.
- Without Him we can do nothing.
- When we abide in Him, we can ask whatever we will, and it shall be done for us.
- Jesus loves us just as the Father loves Him.
- The Father loves us.
- We are to love one another.
- God wants us to have joy and for our joy to be full.
- The Lord no longer calls us servants but friends.

Therefore, any vision or dream about God the Father and God the Son that speaks contrary to the above scripture is not to be received.

The next scriptures tell us about God the Holy Spirit.

John 16:13-15: (When the Spirit of truth comes)

> Howbeit when he, **the Spirit of truth, is come, he will guide you into all truth**: for **he shall not speak of himself**; but **whatsoever he shall hear, that shall he speak**: and **he will shew you things to come.**
> **He shall glorify me: for he shall receive of mine, and shall shew it unto you.**
> All things that the Father hath are mine: therefore said I, that **he shall take of mine, and shall shew it unto you.**

The key points about the Holy Spirit in the above scripture are:
- He is the Spirit of truth.
- He does not speak of Himself.
- He speaks only what He hears the Father speaks.
- He glorifies the Lord Jesus and not Himself.
- He receives from the Lord Jesus and shows it to us.
- He shows us things to come.

Note: Again, discuss the highlighted parts of the above scripture.

We also see how the Godhead feels about us in the above scripture. Therefore, we must not fall into the devil's snare through false visions and dreams. He wants you to blame God for the unpleasant situations or circumstances in your life by telling you lies in visions and dreams. The devil is the counterfeit that we must reject. He wants you to speak of yourself (through pride) constantly, but we know that we must always give the glory to God.

Other Scriptures that tell us how God feels about us are:

John 8:34-36: **(If the Son sets you free, you are free indeed.)**

> Jesus answered them, Verily, verily, I say unto you, **Whosoever committeth sin is the servant of sin.**
> And the **servant abideth not in the house forever: but the Son abideth ever. If the Son therefore shall make you free, ye shall be free indeed.**

Matthew 7:11**(If you know how to give good gifts to your children)**

> If ye then, being evil, know how to give good gifts unto your children, how much more shall **your Father which is in heaven give good things to them that ask him?**

Note: Again, emphasize to the students that God wants us to be free from all bondage and He wants to give us good things. It is the devil that wants to give us bad and evil things. Review the highlighted points in the scriptures below also.

Psalm 84:11 **(The Lord is your shield.)**

> **For the LORD God is a <u>sun</u> and shield:** the LORD will give grace and glory: **no good thing will he withhold from them that walk uprightly.**

1 John 1:5 **(God is Light.)**

> This then is the message which we have heard of him, and declare unto you, that **God is light, and in him is no darkness at all.**

The devil uses ignorance and lack of knowledge in correctly interpreting visions and dreams to deceive people into believing that God is angry with them, or to teach them to always hope and believe in evil reports.

Remember--the devil took the Lord to a pinnacle and showed him all the kingdoms of this world and their glory **(Matthew 4:8.)** It was the devil's evil attempt to make the Lord fall into the sin of idolatry.

The Truth about the Devil

John 8:43-44 **(He is a liar, even in visions and dreams.)**

> Why do ye not understand my speech? Even because ye cannot hear my word. Ye are of your father the devil, and **the lusts of your father ye will do. He was a murderer from the beginning,** and **abode not in the truth, because there is no truth in him. When he speaketh a lie, he speaketh of his own** (he speaks or bear witness of himself)**: for he is a liar, and the father of it.**

Therefore, the devil's dreams are usually coded with lies, evil report and death. The key points to note in the above scripture are:

·   The devil is a murderer.
·   He is a liar and the father of lies.
·   He does not stay (abide) in the truth.
·   There is no truth in him.
·   He inspires his children to perform his lusts or evil desires.

2 Corinthians 11:14-15 **(Transforms himself as an angel of light)**

> And no marvel; for **Satan himself is transformed into an angel of light.**
> Therefore it is no great thing if **his ministers also be transformed as the ministers of righteousness**; whose end shall be according to their works.

Note: Godly dreams will speak of:

1. Promotion and Hope

God desires a future and a hope for us. This always comes forth in the visions and dreams that He gives us. We see this in Jeremiah 29:11 **(Future and Hope).**

For I know the thoughts that I think toward you, says the LORD, thoughts of peace and not of evil, to give you a future and a hope. (NKJV)

God is not withholding anything from us. He wants to bless us. We see this in John 16:23-24 **(Asking in Jesus's Name)**

And in that day ye shall ask me nothing. Verily, verily, I say unto you, Whatsoever ye shall ask the Father in my name, he will give it you. Hitherto have ye asked nothing in my name: ask, and ye shall receive, that your joy may be full.

John 14:14 **(God's willingness to help us)**

If ye shall ask any thing in my name, I will do it.

2. Life

God's will or desire is that we may have life and that we may have it more abundantly. He is not willing that any should perish. He desires for us to receive His Son, Jesus, so that He can give us life.

John 11:25 (The Resurrection and the Life)

> Jesus said unto her, I am the resurrection, and the life: he that believeth in me, though he were dead, yet shall he live: And whosoever liveth and believeth in me shall never die...

John 14:19: (Because I live, ye shall live also.)

> Yet a little while, and the world seeth me no more; but ye see me: because I live, ye shall live also.

3. Harvest/Prosperity

It is God's will that we prosper and have a bountiful harvest.

John 15:8 (Being fruitful)

> Herein is my Father glorified, that ye bear much fruit; so shall ye be my disciples.

Job 33:14-18 (Holy Spirit will warn us.)

The Holy Spirit will warn you about things to come whether good or bad.

> For God speaketh once, yea twice, yet man perceiveth it not. In a dream, in a vision of the night, when deep sleep falleth upon men, in slumberings upon the bed; Then he openeth the ears of men, and sealeth their instruction, that He may withdraw man from his purpose, and hide pride from man. He keepeth back his soul from the pit, and his life from perishing by the sword.

Note: The devil's visions and dreams speak of

1. Failure, lack, famine.
2. Self-promotion and pride and reliance on own strength, e.g., controlling everything.
3. Demotion.
4. Your past evil ways--such as a carnal or ungodly background and old friends that represent your old life—that God erased with the blood of Jesus.
5. Ungodly alliances (watch out for ungodly scenarios in your visions and dreams).

John 7:18 (he that speaks of himself)

> He that speaketh of himself seeketh his own glory: but he that seeketh his glory

that sent him, the same is true, and no unrighteousness is in him.

A classic example of a dream from the devil is found in Job 4:12-21:

> Now **a thing was secretly brought to me**, and mine ear received a little thereof.
> In **thoughts from the visions of the night,** when deep sleep falleth on men,
> **Fear came upon me, and trembling, which made all my bones to shake.**
> Then **a spirit passed before my face; the hair of my flesh stood up:**
> **It stood still, but I could not discern the form thereof: an image was before mine eyes**, there was silence, and I heard a voice, saying,
> **Shall mortal man be more just than God**? Shall a man be more pure than his maker?
> Behold, **he put no trust in his servants**; and **his angels he charged with folly:**
> **How much less in them that dwell in houses of clay**, whose foundation is in the dust, **which are crushed before the moth?**
> They are destroyed from morning to evening: **they perish forever without any regarding it.**
> **Doth not their excellency which is in them, go away? They die, even without wisdom.**

The words spoken by this spirit about God and His people are not true. We will discuss this dream in detail in another class-- **How to Analyze the Contents of Your Visions and Dreams.**

Look at Job's complaints in the scripture below to see how the devil was vexing him with visions. This is a good example of the effect of an evil spirit's work on a person through false visions and dreams.

Job 13:20-27 (**The devil tries to portray God as our enemy or tormentor.**)

> **Only do not two things unto me: then will I not hide myself from thee**
> **Withdraw thine hand far from me**: and **let not thy dread make me afraid.**
> Then call thou, and I will answer: or let me speak, and answer thou me.
> How many are mine iniquities and sins? Make me to know my transgression and my sin.
> **Wherefore hidest thou thy face, and holdest me for thine enemy?**
> Wilt thou break a leaf driven to and fro? and wilt thou pursue the dry stubble?
> **For thou writest bitter things against me, and makest me to possess the iniquities of my youth.**
> **Thou puttest my feet also in the stocks, and lookest narrowly unto all my paths; thou settest a print upon the heels of my feet.**

The devil can pretend to be the Lord as he vexes your soul and spirit. I experienced some of the same torments that Job experienced. In some of my own visions and dreams, the devil has tried to portray himself as the Lord who was punishing me for some evil that I had done. Because I was ignorant of the meaning of salvation, I believed him for a whole year! I kicked him out when

I found out the truth about what the Lord Jesus purchased for me on Calvary.

The devil used to appear in my dreams pretending to be the Lord Jesus. He would dress like Jesus, and with an accordion or guitar or some other musical instrument in his hands, he would play as loudly as he could in my ears to keep me awake. He would laugh and delight himself as I tried to shield my ears from him. I always wondered why the Lord Jesus would take delight in tormenting me until the Lord opened my understanding. As a matter of fact, the Lord told me that the same spirit that afflicted Job was the spirit that was sent against me. The "spirit of the plague of Job" actually comes before you, pretending to be God, while delighting in vexing and tormenting you. I thought that it was Jesus who had become my enemy and was taking great pleasure in tormenting me.

I had to spend some time in the book of Job so I could learn how to defeat this spirit. When the Lord allowed me to discern the spirit as it was departing from me, I saw its true identity for the first time. It was an evil spirit, covered with boils, and had other spirits as helpers.

The Lord then taught me how to discern between the clean and the unclean and between the holy and the profane. After that, I saw that the devil's robes are not always pure and holy. He cannot counterfeit holiness.

Note: Teacher, be sure to point out to the students that God would never do those things that the evil spirit was doing to Job. God is good and God is love.

Note: The extent to which you know and remember the Word of God is the extent to which you can immediately identify and analyze the sources and contents of your visions and dreams. The Holy Spirit uses scriptures to decode visions and dreams for you.

End Teaching Here

Activation
This is the part of the class where you gather the students together and:
- You identify new members in the class who are Spirit-filled and would like to receive the Anointing of skills in visions and dreams.
- You lay hands on them to receive the Anointing.
- You pray for the entire class.

Session on Actual Dreams and Their Interpretations
This is the part of the class where class members share their dreams and everyone believes the Lord for understanding of the dream.

Note:

- All interpretations must be based on scriptures.
- Everyone in the class should be allowed to participate, even if their answers are wrong.
- Listen carefully to identify any error in each answer as the students speak (**use the blank notes at the end of each lesson to record each student's interpretation**).
- Allow everyone to give his or her interpretation before you address each response.
- Identify all inaccurate interpretations and address them.
- Summarize the accurate points that were identified by the students and address any portion of the dream still needing interpretation.

Note: Most students will skip portions of the dream that they do not understand, so be sure to address those portions of the dream.

Below is an actual dream. Examine the different interpretations and see what other revelations you and the students get concerning it.

The Move Dream

I moved into another apartment run by the same management company.
It was a plain building. The main door to the apartment opened onto a deserted street in a downtown area.
Construction was going on, on a huge building across the street.
It was like a dark depressing day; its dark skies made it look like it was going to rain.
After I looked outside, up and down the street, I closed the front door and started unpacking boxes. After a few hours, I walked by to find that the front door had been wide open for hours. I secured it and knew I'd have to lock the two doors leading to the foyer for protection. I was afraid the front door would open again.
I told Pastor Buddy what happened and he wanted to know the name of the street.
I was walking down the deserted street looking for the name, and finally came to my door. When I found it, I tried to open it, but the doorknob came off in my hand.

Interpretations

Note: Mary examines the interpretations given by the students and makes comments. Her comments to each student are in **boldface.** The *italicized words* are the student's words that Mary addressed.

Note: Teacher, pay attention to how each dream was interpreted by the students. Use the same approach to get your students to do the same.

Janis's Interpretation

These are key phrases or words that I received as being significant: run by the same management; door opened; construction; I closed the front door; unpacking boxes; the front door had been wide open to receive; afraid.

There was something from the past (unpacking boxes) that the enemy wants to use as a means of access to keep her in a dark place. Doors had been left open for the enemy's entrance, but as a result of the work (construction) that the Lord is doing, there will no longer be access for the enemy. Pastor Buddy represents God causing her to leave the place (state of mind) where she was so He can make sure that she cannot go back.

Scripture: **Therefore, if the Son sets you free, you shall be free indeed**-- John 8:36.

There was something from the past (unpacking boxes) that the enemy wants to use as a means of access to keep her in a dark place. **Instructor: Very good, Janis.** *Doors had been left open for the enemy's entrance, but as a result of the work (construction) that the Lord is doing, there will no longer be access for the enemy.* **Instructor: There is nothing about the construction going on across the street that tied it to the Lord. Therefore, we cannot ascribe the construction to the Lord.**

Pastor Buddy represents God causing her to leave the place (state of mind) where she was so that He can make sure that she cannot go back. **Instructor: Very good! Yes, the man of God is trying to get her to have knowledge concerning her environment. Yes, it could be her mind.**

Scripture: Therefore, if the Son sets you free, you shall be free indeed--John 8: 36

Instructor: **She still needs to be set free because the doorknob came off in her hand.**

Misa's Interpretation

Since the move was a lateral move-- no upgrades, no new management-- it is something that she needs to watch out for. God always promotes, and He should be the management. Also, impending storms and open doors are a clear warning that this move is not from the Lord.

I would give it back to its source and claim and confess only divine promotion.

Instructor: Very good, Misa, but you could have pressed deeper for more revelation for the other portions of the dream.

I would give it back to its source and claim and confess only divine promotion.

Instructor: Yes, she needs to cancel the dream. It does not speak life or protection.

Robin's Interpretation

Be still and know that I AM GOD...

Daughter, know I have not called you to move from the place where you are now, but the enemy desires to move to you into a place I have not called you into. He has steered your focus to paths that would lead to desolation and despair. Daughter, redirect your focus beyond what the enemy has shown you and see that I am rebuilding those areas in your life. You are looking for closure so you can begin to sort things out. In times past, you have tried to secure these areas, only to see you were still vulnerable and fearful. Daughter, know that this is a new day and that old things are passed away. Behold, all things have become new.

Be still and know that I AM GOD…

Daughter, know I have not called you to move from the place were you are now, but the enemy desires to move to you into a place I have not called you into. He has steered your focus to paths that would lead to desolation and despair. Daughter, redirect your focus beyond what the enemy has shown you and see that I am rebuilding those areas in your life. You are looking for closure so you can begin to sort things out. In times past, you have tried to secure these areas, only to see you were still vulnerable and fearful. Daughter, know that this is a new day and that old things are passed away. Behold, all things have become new. **Instructor: Thanks, Robin. You got the gist of the dream, but you are giving her a prophetic word instead of telling her the meaning of her dream. This word of exhortation and encouragement should come after you interpret the dream. This is not a dream to be embraced by her.**

Anita's Interpretation:

Hi, Everyone!! …I first have some questions for the dreamer that may really be leading towards searching or re-evaluating of some issues. 1.) Is this dream concerning your job? 2.) Are you looking at job changing? 3.) Are things changing from what their standard once was?

The move to the other apartment was not an upgrade, no next level, no promotion.

The building was plain- you feel unnoticed or passed over. The main door opens to a deserted street in a downtown area--feelings of being the only one, or aloneness, in nowhere of importance. There is some emptiness. Yet, you can see construction going on in a huge building across the street--symbolizing new things. Promotion for others, are just across the way (which is reachable!) The huge building represents BIG THINGS. If you would go over, there is a place for you. The condition of the weather would lead you to think nothing good is going to happen, but remember, the best is yet to come!! Do not settle for okay; bring your expectations up high in spite of past experiences, unexplained things or questions as to why. You have done what you could to the best of your ability. God has not forgotten you!! Do not allow spirits of unsure-ness, uncertainty, to come in and let not your trust be lost. God's plan for you is GOOD. Promotion is your portion. I think the question Pastor Buddy asked is a very good one…What is the name of the street?

Fear is the name, only you could not see it because it was wrapped in so many other disguises. But the root of what the enemy is to send fear. You do have access to the door of promotion. The knob to that door will not come off in your hands--You will move FORWARD!!!

Instructor: Anita, You need to pay attention to the dream and not the dreamer. *"Hi, Everyone!! …I first have some questions for the dreamer that may really be leading towards searching or re-evaluating of some issues. 1.) Is this dream concerning your job? 2.) Are you looking at job changing? 3.) Are things changing from what their standard once was?"* **Instructor: You asked too many questions about her natural state.**

The move to the other apartment was not an upgrade, no next level, no promotion. The building was plain- you feel unnoticed or passed over. The main door opens to a deserted street in a downtown area--feelings of being the only one, or aloneness, in nowhere of importance. There is some emptiness. **Instructor: Very good Anita.**

Yet, you can see construction going on in a huge building across the street--symbolizing new things. Promotion for others, are just across the way (which is reachable!) The huge building represents BIG THINGS. If you would go over, there is a place for you. **Instructor: Nothing in the dream tells us the nature of the construction across the street. It could be good or bad.**

The condition of the weather would lead you to think nothing good is going to happen, but remember, the best is yet to come!! **We cannot accept the evil report of the bad weather, the street and the doors.**

Do not settle for okay; bring your expectations up high in spite of past experiences, unexplained things or questions as to why. You have done what you could to the best of your ability. God has not forgotten you!! Do not allow spirits of unsure-ness, uncertainty, to come in and let not your trust be lost. God's plan for you is GOOD. Promotion is your portion. **Instructor: You did not encourage her not to receive the dream! The dream is an evil report from the enemy.**

I think the question Pastor Buddy asked is a very good one...What is the name of the street...? **Instructor: This is good, Anita. It is like God asking Adam, "Where are you, Adam?"**

*Fear is the name, only you could not see it because it was wrapped in so many other disguises. But the root of what the enemy is to send fear. You do have access to the door of promotion. The knob to that door will not come off in your hands--***Instructor: Since there is fear and disaster with the door knob, you should tell her not to accept this dream.**

You will move FORWARD!!! **Instructor: Finally, Anita, you do not need to ask questions about her physical situation because that might color your interpretation. You may ask questions that will clarify the contents of the dream, but not about the dreamer's physical condition or situation. Also, do not give someone a homework assignment with a lot of questions when you are given a dream to interpret. Analyze the dream only.**

Mary's Comments

This is not a good dream, despite all of the good points that you all have highlighted. Yes--there was no promotion, but a gloomy, dark, depressing day and doors that would not stay closed. Yes--boxes represent things from the past that she had put away, but the devil is trying to get her to unpack them. The dreamer lacks knowledge of her own environment and this in itself is not good. The Lord always gives us spiritual discernment. He that walks with Jesus does not walk in darkness.

Basically, this is a classic dream from the devil designed to give the illusion of promotion (moving to another apartment), but it is mixed with some evil reports about her living condition and her environment.

I would tell the dreamer to cancel the dream and declare that the devil's evil report will not stand because of the blood of Jesus. Then, she needs to repent for anything she has done to open the door for the devil to show her this dream. She needs to confess the salvation, protection and promotion that she has in the Lord Jesus.

Yes, let her send the dream back to the devil that crafted it!

Note: Teacher, instruct the students to watch out for the subtle and well-crafted lies of the devil in visions and dreams. A lie is not always the opposite of the truth. Sometimes, it is truth peppered with subtle lies.

Teacher's Notes and Students' Comments

Teacher's Notes and Students' Comments

Teacher's Notes and Students' Comments

Teacher's Notes and Students' Comments

Teacher's Notes and Students' Comments

LESSON 4

Type of Visions and Dreams

1. Literal Visions and Dreams

Webster's Dictionary defines literal as:

- *In accordance with*
- *Exact meaning*
- *Word for word (strict)*
- *Restricted to fact (precise)*

God's dreams are sometimes very literal as He wants us to get the exact point or instructions that He has for us. Most of the visions and dreams that He gives us are literal.

NOTE: God used literal dreams to intervene in the circumstances surrounding baby Jesus's birth. We see this in Matthew 1:20:

> **But while he thought on these things, behold the Angel of the Lord appeared unto him in a dream saying Joseph thou son of David, fear not to take unto thee Mary thy wife; for that which is conceived in her is of the Holy Ghost.**

NOTE: God clears up the situation between Mary and Joseph. Joseph would not have married Mary without God's divine intervention through a dream.

The following scriptures also show how God uses dreams to warn and instruct us.

1. Matthew 2:12:
And being warned of God in a dream that they should not return to Herod, they departed into their own country another way.

2. Matthew 2:13:
When they were departed, the Angel of the Lord appeared to Joseph in a dream saying, Arise, and take the young child and his mother, and flee into Egypt and be thou there until I bring thee word.

3. Matthew 2:19-20:
But when Herod was dead, behold, an angel of the Lord appeared in a dream to Joseph in Egypt, saying, Arise, and take the young child and his mother, and go into the land of Israel: for they are dead which sought the young child's life.

4. Matthew 2:22-23 **(Due to being warned in a dream, Joseph turned aside into Galilee)**
But when he heard that Archelaus did reign in Judea in the room of his father Herod, he was afraid to go thither: notwithstanding, being warned of God in a dream, he turned aside into the parts of Galilee: And he came and dwelt in a city called Nazareth: that it might be fulfilled which was spoken by the prophets, He shall be called a Nazarene.

NOTE: God used a literal vision to confirm and affirm the Lord Jesus as His Son, the Messiah, to John the Baptist. God told John the Baptist to watch for something that would happen during baptism: There would be a sign that would help him to identify the Messiah.

The scriptures are:

1. John 1:29-34 **(God confirms Jesus to John)**

The next day John seeth Jesus coming unto him, and saith, Behold the Lamb of God, which taketh away the sin of the world. This is he of whom I said, After me cometh a man which is preferred before me: for he was before me. And I knew him not: but that he should be made manifest to Israel, therefore am I come baptizing with water. And John bare record, saying, **I saw the Spirit descending from heaven like a dove, and it abode upon him.** And I knew him not: but he that sent me to baptize with water, the same said unto me, **Upon whom thou shalt see the Spirit descending, and remaining on him,** the same is he which baptized with the Holy Ghost. **And I saw, and bare record that this is the Son of God.**

2. Matthew 3:16-17 **(God confirms His Son)**

And Jesus, when he was baptized, went up straightway out of the water: and, lo, the heavens were opened unto him, and **he saw the Spirit of God descending like a dove, and lighting upon him:** And lo a voice from heaven, saying, This is my beloved Son, in whom I am well pleased.

Other Literal Visions
(Class discussion of the following visions is optional)

Acts 9:1-6 **(Saul's conversion to Christianity = literal vision/encounter)**

And Saul, yet breathing out threatening and slaughter against the disciples of the Lord, went unto the high priest. And desired of him letters to Damascus to the synagogues, that if he found any of this way, whether they were men or women, he might bring them bound unto Jerusalem. And as he journeyed, he came near Damascus: and **suddenly there shined round about him a light from heaven: And he fell to the earth, and heard a voice saying unto him, Saul, Saul, why persecutest thou me?** And he said, Who art thou, Lord? And the Lord said, I am Jesus whom thou persecutest: it is hard for thee to kick against the pricks. And he trembling and astonished said, Lord, what wilt thou have me to do? And the Lord said unto him, Arise, and go into the city, and it shall be told thee what thou must do.

Acts 22:17-18 **(Paul warned to leave Jerusalem)**
And it came to pass, that, when I was come again to Jerusalem, even while I prayed in the temple, **I was in a trance; And saw him saying unto me, Make haste, and get thee quickly out of Jerusalem:** for they will not receive thy testimony concerning me.

Acts 18 9-10 **(Speak and be not afraid to speak)**
Then spake the Lord to Paul in the night by a vision, Be not afraid, but speak, and hold not thy peace: For I am with thee, and no man shall set on thee to hurt thee: for I have much

people in this city.

Acts 23:11 (**The Lord stood by Paul at night and told him to be of good cheer**)
And the night following the Lord stood by him, and said, Be of good cheer, Paul: for as thou hast testified of me in Jerusalem, so must thou bear witness also at Rome.

Acts 9:12 (**Ananias is sent to Saul to restore his sight**)
And hath seen in a vision a man named, Ananias coming in, and putting his hand on him, that he might receive his sight.

2. Symbolic or Representative Visions and Dreams
The second kind of visions and dreams is the symbolic or representative type.
God sometimes uses images, symbols and objects to get His message across to us. The following scriptures show us how God used objects as symbols and images in visions and dreams.

    A. **Genesis 37:6-8:** Joseph's dream of sheaves.
        Sheaves = Joseph and his brothers.
    B. **Genesis 37:9-11:** Joseph's second dreams of the sun and the moon. Sun and Moon = Joseph's father and stepmother.
    C. **Genesis 41:1-7:** Seven Cows = Seven years of plenty and seven years of famine. Seven ears of corn = Seven years of plenty and seven years of famine.
    D. **Daniel 8:2-12:** Daniel's dream of rams and goats
        (Daniel 8:19-23 gives us the explanation of the dream.)
    E. **Daniel 2:31-35:** Daniel's dream of the image of Nebuchadnezzar
    F. **Acts 10:11-16:** Peter's vision of a vessel descending from heaven containing all manner of four-footed beasts. (Acts 10:28-29 = The Gentiles).
    G. **Revelations 6:1-11:** The beast, horses and white robes.

Note: Teacher, be sure to inform the students that it takes divine wisdom to know what the symbols and images represent in visions and dreams. This is why receiving the Anointing for skills and understanding in visions and dreams is vital. God is the interpreter of visions and dreams and He uses us as vessels to deliver the message.

3. Similitude Visions and Dreams
Similitude is a word that we do not hear much in Christendom, but it is a vital tool that God uses in visions and dreams.

Webster's dictionary defines similitude as:
    • *The quality or state of being similar*
    • *Something closely resembling another*
Hosea 12:10:

I have also spoken by the prophets, and I have multiplied visions, and used <u>similitudes</u>, by the ministry of the prophets

Example of a Similitude

The Macedonia Call--**Acts 16:9-15:**

> During the night Paul had **a vision of a man of Macedonia standing and begging him, "Come over to Macedonia and help us.** After Paul had seen the vision, we got ready at once to leave for Macedonia, **concluding that God had called us to preach the gospel to them.** From Troas we put out to sea and sailed straight for Samothrace, and the next day on to Neapolis. From there we traveled to Philippi, a Roman colony and the leading city of that district of Macedonia. And we stayed there several days. On the Sabbath we went outside the city gate to the river, where we expected to find a place of prayer. **We sat down and began to speak to the women who had gathered there. One of those listening was a woman named Lydia, a dealer in purple cloth from the city of Thyatira, who was a worshiper of God. The Lord opened her heart to respond to Paul's message.** When she and the members of her household were baptized, **she invited us to her home. "If you consider me a believer in the Lord,"** she said, **"come and stay at my house." And she persuaded us.**

Note: Paul saw a man in his vision giving him what we now call the "Macedonia Call," but when he got to Macedonia, it was a woman that actually placed the demand on him to come to her house! This is a similitude. The man and the woman are similar in that they are both Christians (believers). So, in effect, the man that Paul saw in his vision was only representing the believers in Macedonia, of which the woman is one.

- *Paul saw a picture of a man = Believer*
- *But they stayed with a woman=Believer*

This is why you sometimes see people who are not naturally members of your family acting in your visions or dreams as your mother, father, brother, sister, cousins and in-laws or church brethren. The similitude would then be the type of **relationship**.

4. Interactive Visions Dreams

Another kind of visions and dreams is the interactive vision or interactive dream.

Definition: Interactive = A source of both input and output

Interact = To act on each other

- They are different from a physical visitation but are very similar because you see and interact with God the Father, the Lord Jesus Christ, the Holy Ghost, the angels etc...

- A visitation is when God literally walks into your room, office, or <u>wherever</u> you happen to be.

- In an interactive vision or dream, the Lord engages you in an ongoing conversation.

My personal example of an interactive vision:
In my book, <u>Unveiling the God-Mother</u>, (pp. 63-64), I talked about how, during a church service, God the Father and God the Son appeared to me in a vision in a little neighborhood church.

Excerpt from <u>Unveiling the God-Mother</u>*:*

On my first Sunday back in the United States from Nigeria, I decided to attend the little church in the neighborhood where I lived. It was my second Sunday as a true Christian so I was up bright and early. I was probably the second or third person to show up for service but I was not prepared for what was to happen to me on this day. As people began to come inside the church for service, I noticed that they would go and sit in other pews away from me. Eventually the church was full and I noticed that people preferred to stand in the isle rather than sit on the same pew with me. I was the only black person in the congregation on this Sunday, so my initial reaction was to tell myself that I did not need them and walk out of the place, but because I am not one to give up or run from a fight, I decided to stay, but the exit lights were all the time very visible to me.

The priest began the service and I thought, how hypocritical for these people to preach love and act the way they were acting toward me. A sudden resolve not to get angry or pay attention to what was happening came over me and I began to participate in the service. I was determined not to let anyone dampen my new enthusiasm for my Lord and Savior Jesus Christ. When the service got to the part where the congregation had to join the priest to recite the Creed, and as I opened my mouth to say the Creed also, tears began to flow down my cheeks. *Then, all of a sudden heaven opened and I began to see God the Father and the Lord Jesus sitting on the throne above the congregation. God the Father said to me, "It is me you came for isn't it?" and I said, "Yes," and He said, "Then, wipe away the tears from your eyes and look unto me alone."* I wiped my eyes and I again joined the service. This is how I received the gift of interaction with the Lord in conversations. Since this incident, and from that day, I could ask the Lord a question and He would give me an immediate answer!

Here is **another example of an interactive vision** that I had:

In a vision, I saw the devil drag a big, black plastic trash bag into my bedroom. I watched him empty the contents of the trash bag onto the floor. I noticed that the items were audiocassette tapes. He sat down, and with great pride, began to slowly roll up his sleeves. When he was done, he began digging among the tapes for a particular tape. As I wondered why he was deliberately searching for one tape, I became aware that God the Father was also on the scene. He was watching me as I was watching the devil. I knew that the devil was not aware that God the Father was around. I turned to God the Father and asked Him what the tapes represented. I also asked Him why the devil was looking for a particular tape. He said to me, "Oh, the tapes are your past. He is looking for the right tape that he thinks might drive you out of your mind." I said to God the Father, "So what do I do?" He replied, "Just remind him that the cross of Jesus Christ is now your past."

I then turned to the devil and said to him, "My God said to remind you that the cross of Jesus Christ is now my past." He got very furious and quickly gathered his tapes back into the trash bag.

117

The devil does not like to be put to shame so he could not wait to quickly depart with his tapes. As he was dragging the bag of tapes away, God the Father leaned backward on His throne and began to clap His hands and laugh. I joined Him in clapping and laughing as we both watched the devil depart in shame.

Note: Interactive visions can be very real.

Examples of Interactive Visions in the Scriptures

Ezekiel 37:1-4 **(Prophesying to the Dry Bones)**

> **The hand of the LORD was upon me, and carried me out in the spirit of the LORD, and set me down in the midst of the valley which was full of bones, And caused me to pass by them round about: and, behold, there were very many in the open valley; and, lo, they were very dry.**
> **And he said unto me, Son of man, can these bones live? And I answered, O Lord GOD, thou knowest.**
> **Again he said unto me, Prophesy upon these bones, and say unto them, O ye dry bones, hear the word of the LORD.**

Jeremiah 1:11-14 **(About Seeing)**

> **Moreover the word of the LORD came unto me, saying, Jeremiah, what seest thou? And I said, I see a rod of an almond tree.**
> **Then said the LORD unto me, Thou hast well seen: for I will hasten my word to perform it.**
> **And the word of the LORD came unto me the second time, saying, What seest thou? And I said, I see a seething pot; and the face thereof is toward the north.**
> **Then the LORD said unto me, Out of the north an evil shall break forth upon all the inhabitants of the land.**

Acts 9:1-8: **(About Paul)**

> **And Saul, yet breathing out threatening and slaughter against the disciples of the Lord, went unto the high priest,**
> **And desired of him letters to Damascus to the synagogues, that if he found any of this way, whether they were men or women, he might bring them bound unto Jerusalem.**
> **And as he journeyed, he came near Damascus: and suddenly there shined round about him a light from heaven:**
> **And he fell to the earth, and heard a voice saying unto him, Saul, Saul, why persecutest thou me?**

And he said, Who art thou, Lord? And the Lord said, I am Jesus whom thou persecutest: it is hard for thee to kick against the pricks.

And he trembling and astonished said, Lord, what wilt thou have me to do? And the Lord said unto him, Arise, and go into the city, and it shall be told thee what thou must do.

And the men which journeyed with him stood speechless, hearing a voice, but seeing no man.

And Saul arose from the earth; and when his eyes were opened, he saw no man: but they led him by the hand, and brought him into Damascus.

Acts 9:10-18 (Ananias being sent to Saul)

And there was a certain disciple at Damascus, named Ananias; and to him said the Lord in a vision, Ananias. And he said, Behold, I am here, Lord.

And the Lord said unto him, Arise, and go into the street which is called Straight, and enquire in the house of Judas for one called Saul, of Tarsus: for, behold, he prayeth,

And hath seen in a vision a man named Ananias coming in, and putting his hand on him, that he might receive his sight.

Then Ananias answered, Lord, I have heard by many of this man, how much evil he hath done to thy saints at Jerusalem:

And here he hath authority from the chief priests to bind all that call on thy name.

But the Lord said unto him, Go thy way: for he is a chosen vessel unto me, to bear my name before the Gentiles, and kings, and the children of Israel:

For I will shew him how great things he must suffer for my name's sake.

And Ananias went his way, and entered into the house; and putting his hands on him said, Brother Saul, the Lord, even Jesus, that appeared unto thee in the way as thou camest, hath sent me, that thou mightest receive thy sight, and be filled with the Holy Ghost.

And immediately there fell from his eyes as it had been scales: and he received sight forthwith, and arose, and was baptized.

5. Visitation

Webster's Dictionary defines **visitation** as:
- **An act of visiting or an instance of being visited.**
- **A visit for the purpose of making an official inspection or examination.**
- **The arrival or appearance of a supernatural being.**

It is the last definition that we are talking about when we speak of a divine visitation.

Note: Visitations are also ways that the Lord speaks to His people.

Moses by the burning bush

Exodus 3:2-10:

> And the angel of the LORD appeared unto him in a flame of fire out of the midst of a bush: and he looked, and, behold, the bush burned with fire, and the bush was not consumed.
>
> And Moses said, I will now turn aside, and see this great sight, why the bush is not burnt.
>
> And when the LORD saw that he turned aside to see, God called unto him out of the midst of the bush, and said, Moses, Moses. And he said, Here am I.
>
> And he said, Draw not nigh hither: put off thy shoes from off thy feet, for the place whereon thou standest is holy ground.
>
> Moreover he said, I am the God of thy father, the God of Abraham, the God of Isaac, and the God of Jacob. And Moses hid his face; for he was afraid to look upon God.
>
> And the LORD said, I have surely seen the affliction of my people which are in Egypt, and have heard their cry by reason of their taskmasters; for I know their sorrows;
>
> And I am come down to deliver them out of the hand of the Egyptians, and to bring them up out of that land unto a good land and a large, unto a land flowing with milk and honey; unto the place of the Canaanites, and the Hittites, and the Amorites, and the Perizzites, and the Hivites, and the Jebusites.
>
> Now therefore, behold, the cry of the children of Israel is come unto me: and I have also seen the oppression wherewith the Egyptians oppress them.
>
> Come now therefore, and I will send thee unto Pharaoh, that thou mayest bring forth my people the children of Israel out of Egypt.

The book of Job contains a very good example of a divine visitation. Job had levied many charges against God in the time of his affliction. God showed up personally to set the record straight. Review the following scriptures.

Job 38:1-4:

> Then the LORD answered Job out of the whirlwind, and said,
> Who is this that darkeneth counsel by words without knowledge?
> Gird up now thy loins like a man; for I will demand of thee, and answer thou me.
> Where wast thou when I laid the foundations of the earth? declare, if thou hast understanding.

Job 40:6-14:

> Then answered the LORD unto Job out of the whirlwind, and said,
> Gird up thy loins now like a man: I will demand of thee, and declare thou unto

me.

Wilt thou also disannul my judgment? wilt thou condemn me, that thou mayest be righteous?

Hast thou an arm like God? or canst thou thunder with a voice like him?

Deck thyself now with majesty and excellency; and array thyself with glory and beauty.

Cast abroad the rage of thy wrath: and behold every one that is proud, and abase him.

Look on every one that is proud, and bring him low; and tread down the wicked in their place.

Hide them in the dust together; and bind their faces in secret.

Then will I also confess unto thee that thine own right hand can save thee.

Job 42: 1-6:

Then Job answered the LORD, and said,

I know that thou canst do every thing, and that no thought can be withholden from thee.

Who is he that hideth counsel without knowledge? therefore have I uttered that I understood not; things too wonderful for me, which I knew not.

Hear, I beseech thee, and I will speak: I will demand of thee, and declare thou unto me.

I have heard of thee by the hearing of the ear: <u>but now mine eye seeth thee.</u>

Wherefore I abhor myself, and repent in dust and ashes.

Note: In the book of Revelation, John saw the Lord right before his eyes.

Rev 1:10-19:

I was in the Spirit on the Lord's day, and heard behind me a great voice, as of a trumpet,

Saying, I am Alpha and Omega, the first and the last: and, What thou seest, write in a book, and send it unto the seven churches which are in Asia; unto Ephesus, and unto Smyrna, and unto Pergamos, and unto Thyatira, and unto Sardis, and unto Philadelphia, and unto Laodicea.

And I turned to see the voice that spake with me. And being turned, I saw seven golden candlesticks;

And in the midst of the seven candlesticks one like unto the Son of man, clothed with a garment down to the foot, and girt about the paps with a golden girdle.

His head and his hairs were white like wool, as white as snow; and his eyes were as a flame of fire;

And his feet like unto fine brass, as if they burned in a furnace; and his voice as the sound of many waters.

And he had in his right hand seven stars: and out of his mouth went a sharp two-edged sword: and his countenance was as the sun shineth in his strength.
And when I saw him, I fell at his feet as dead. And he laid his right hand upon me, saying unto me, Fear not; I am the first and the last:
I am he that liveth, and was dead; and, behold, I am alive for evermore, Amen; and have the keys of hell and of death.
Write the things which thou hast seen, and the things which are, and the things which shall be hereafter;

NOTE: You can also get the word of the LORD without seeing a vision. God can just talk to you! He spoke to Samuel by calling Samuel's name.

God spoke to Jeremiah without showing him any vision

Jeremiah 36:1-3:

And it came to pass in the fourth year of Jehoiakim the son of Josiah king of Judah, that this word came unto Jeremiah from the LORD, saying, Take thee a roll of a book, and write therein all the words that I have spoken unto thee against Israel, and against Judah, and against all the nations, from the day I spake unto thee, from the days of Josiah, even unto this day. It may be that the house of Judah will hear all the evil which I purpose to do unto them; that they may return every man from his evil way; that I may forgive their iniquity and their sin.

End Teaching Here

Activation
This is the part of the class where you gather the students together and:
- You identify new members in the class who are Spirit-filled and would like to receive the anointing of skills in visions and dreams.
- You lay hands on them to receive the Anointing.
- You pray for the entire class.

Session on Actual Dreams and Their Interpretations
This is the part of the class where class members share their visions and dreams and everyone extents their faith to the Lord for understanding of the visions or dreams.

Note:
- All interpretations must be based on scriptures.
- Everyone in the class should be allowed to participate even if their answers are wrong.

- Listen carefully to identify any error in each answer as the students speak (use the blank notes at the end of each lesson to record each student's interpretation).
- Allow everyone to give his or her interpretation before you address each response,
- Identify all inaccurate interpretations and address them,
- Summarize the accurate points that were identified by the students and address any portion of the dream still needing interpretation.

Note: Most students will skip portions of the dream that they do not understand, so be sure to address those portions of the dream.

Below is an actual dream. Examine the different interpretations and see what other revelations you and the students receive concerning it.

Family Get-together Dream

My dream scenario: I was at a family get together at the home of an <u>unknown family member</u>. The house was <u>not familiar</u>. Not long after being there, my second <u>oldest brother (who is deceased)</u> came in with his wife and three daughters. I saw them come in and he took a seat next to his wife. <u>Everyone was talking but no one</u> <u>was talking to my brother</u>. I finished my conversation with whoever I was talking to and went over to greet my brother. After saying hello to him, I remembered that he was deceased. I immediately backed away from him and asked, "What are your doing here? You're dead." At that point I woke up.

Interpretations
Note: Mary's comments are **in boldface**. The *italicized words* are the student's words that Mary addressed.

Misa's Interpretation
It appears that the only significant occurrence in the dream was your deceased brother. Even in your dream you realized that something was very wrong with the fact that he was present at a rather odd gathering in a strange house. Cancel the dream. Refuse to have anything with the spirit that appeared in the form of your brother. We live and die once.

Instructor: Excellent, Misa. Yes, we live and die once. We do not communicate or interact with the dead! You did very well with your interpretation.

Anita's Interpretation
The place that you were at was unknown and the relative was unknown to you also. It was not familiar, but the person that looked like your brother was a familiar spirit-- that is why no one saw him. Tell the devil that you don't receive this lie and close any doors that may have been open to having fellowship with the dead (demon imposters). Renounce those things as you did in the dream.

Instructor: Awesome, Anita! You got it. You nailed that familiar spirit and the open door. I could not have said it better.

Janis's Interpretation

I believe that the dream is from the enemy because of the unfamiliarity of the location and the attempt to get you to converse with someone who has passed on. He seems to be trying to get you back into agreement with things that have since been dead or cancelled, etc. by playing on emotion, sentimentalism, etc. and derail you into occultism through necromancy. I counsel you to cancel this dream and leave what is dead to the dead.

Instructor: Way to go, Janis! Yes, whenever there is lack of understanding or discernment in a dream, you have to pay close attention because it will point you immediately to the devil as the one at work in the dream. You got the name of the spirit--"necromancy"-- that is trying to insinuate itself into this person's life. Yes, he needs to cancel the dream.

Robin's Interpretation

This was a dream of warning. God allowed you to see how the enemy (death) is trying to find a way back into your family line by operating through a familiar spirit that came in the form of your deceased brother. You have the authority to cancel the plans of death being assigned to destroy your family members. Break all generational ties with death and all evil covenants from the past in your family. Line up with and speak God's Word of life over your family. Remember: Life and death are in the power of the tongue.

Instructor: Oh, this is very good, Robin. You saw the tactics of the enemy against this person in the dream! Not only did you expose the enemy, but you also gave wise counsel to him to speak the Word of life.

Mary's Comments

You all did so well with the interpretation of this dream. I am so glad to see the level of understanding that you all currently possess as visions and dreams interpreters. Praise the Lord and I give Him all the Glory. He is our teacher.

Teacher's Notes and Students' Comments

Teacher's Notes and Students' Comments

Teacher's Notes and Students' Comments

Teacher's Notes and Students' Comments

LESSON 5

How to Analyze the Contents of Your Visions and Dreams

As I stated before, visions and dreams are God's tools of communication with His people. Therefore, He will code His visions and dreams so that "a picture speaks a thousand words." The devil also crafts his visions and dreams in a way to make people think that they are good, godly and noble. Therefore, it is our duty to identify whose handwriting or signature is on a vision or dream.

To do this, we must know the Word of God. We must study the Word of God as Timothy was instructed in 2 Timothy 2:15:

> Study to shew thyself approved unto God, a workman that needeth not to be ashamed, **rightly dividing the Word of truth.**

The emphasis is on "rightly dividing the Word of truth." This brings us back to the points that we highlighted in Lesson 3--**How to Identify the Sources of Your Visions and Dreams.** We talked about being able to distinguish the counterfeit from the real. This means that you must first be able to identify the source of your vision or dream before addressing its contents.

You must always remember that God the Father, God the Son and God the Holy Spirit love you. They want you to have life, good health, prosperity, peace, joy, and a bountiful harvest.

Therefore, when you have a vision or a dream, you should test it with the Word of God to determine the following:

·   Is it from God, the devil or yourself?
·   Does it speak life, health, promotion, prosperity, etc. into your life?
·   Does it encourage or discourage you?
·   Is it speaking death, lack, destruction, chaos, demotion, loss of something valuable, etc.?
·   Are you in gray, cloudy or dark surroundings?
·   Are you being pursued by some entity?
·   Are you able to see or discern (understand) what is going on in the vision or dream?

Answers to these questions can quickly help you to understand the source of the vision or dream. We know that the Word of God has identified the good things that God has already given to us. Some of them are:

·   Gold
·   Diamonds
·   Silver
·   Children and a good pregnancy   (Please note: There are evil pregnancies in visions and dreams as well)
·   Grapes
·   Fruits
·   Dew
·   Clouds
·   Showers or rainfall
·   Land/houses
·   Favor with God and man
·   Building/temple

- Horn
- Anointing oil or olive oil

These things, when **shown to you in a good setting** in visions and dreams, would usually let you know that God is the one speaking to you.

The devil, on the other hand, wants you to speak against yourself by sending you visions or dreams in which you see **yourself** (this is really not you but a familiar spirit pretending to be you) in an evil surrounding. He uses things like:

- Storms
- Disasters
- Accidents (Note: God can warn you in a vision or dream about the devil's plans to cause an accident. But in the dream, He would not let evil reign)
- War
- Fear
- Black clothing
- Mourning
- Empty basket (no harvest)
- Old buddies or friends and you enjoying your old, evil ways
- You as an instrument of destruction, e.g., setting off a bomb, blowing up a building or killing people.

This list is by no means exhausted here. It is only designed to help you pinpoint what the vision or the dream is saying to you. How God uses the things on this list depends on what He wants to communicate. God can use these things to bless, judge, correct, instruct and warn His people. This is why it is dangerous to run to a book to get the meaning of your vision or dream. What God is trying to communicate to you might be different from what He spoke to the person who wrote the book. You might see the same images as the author of the book, but the message they communicate might be different. Every vision or dream is unique and must be treated as such.

Let us look again at the scripture in Job 4:12-21. This scripture shows us how a spirit can speak and what is spoken does not line up with God's Word. In testing every spirit, you have to make sure that it is the Spirit of the Lord that is speaking. You must also be careful that the spirit that is speaking does not give you a little truth, and then try to sidetrack or derail you by getting you into things that are not true. In this scripture, the spirit started out speaking like it was the Spirit of God. But, as you read on, you discover that it was saying things that are not true about God and us. Let us look closely at the spirit in Job 4:12-21:

Now a word was secretly brought to me and my ear received a whisper of it, In **disquieting thoughts from the visions of the night,** when deep sleep falls on men **fear came upon me, and trembling, which made all my bones shake.** Then a **spirit passed before my face; The hair on my body stood up. It stood still but I could not discern its appearance.** A form was before my eyes; There was silence then I heard a voice saying, "**Can a mortal be more righteous than God? Can a man be more pure than his maker? If he puts no trust in his servants, if he charges his angels with error;** How much more those who dwell in houses of clay whose foundation is in the dust, who are crushed before a moth. **They are broken**

in pieces from morning till evening. They perish forever with no one regarding.
Does not their own excellence go away. **They die even without wisdom."**

Do you see how the content of your dream tell you who is speaking? This spirit that came to this man made his hair to stand up, brought fear to him. The Bible says that God has not given us the spirit of fear. This man could not discern the truth.

The question you must ask is, "What type of spirit is this?" When you listen to what a spirit is saying, you can identify it by the Word of God. This spirit that came to Job's friend says that God charges his angels with error and that God's people die without wisdom and no one regarding. The spirit makes all theses charges against God that we know are contrary to Him.

When you use the Word of the Lord to test this particular spirit, you find that it is not speaking the truth as to who we are from God's perspective. God does not want people to perish. Jesus said, "The son of man has come to seek and to save that which was lost." The Bible further tells us that, "For God so loved the world." This spirit says that no one regards God's people, and "their excellency go away and they die without wisdom." It says, "They perish forever without any regarding." This is not true because God cares. Scripture says that He is not willing that any should perish.

It is not enough for you to hear a spirit speak to you. You must also test the spirit with the Word of the Lord to determine what type of spirit it is. It is not enough for you to see a picture; you need to look at the context of what you are seeing and apply the Word of the Lord to it also to see if it stands that test. This scripture shows us that what this spirit is saying is not true.

Note: Instructor, please ask this question and continue with the following explanation.
"Is there any person in this room that thinks this spirit speaks the truth?"

By the Word of the Lord, it is clear that this spirit does not speak the truth. In the same way that you think about what you hear, and ponder what you see, also meditate on scriptures. To me, this is Visions and Dreams Interpretation 101. Here is a spirit that spoke to this man of God. The man was not a novice in the things of God, but he could not discern spiritually. This man is one of the people who rebuked Job. But, you see the extent and level of his revelation and discernment.

If I had this kind of vision or dream, I would wake up and rebuke the spirit. We have the Holy Spirit now in a way that the Old Testament believers did not have in the beginning. The Lord said that of all those that **were born of women**, John the Baptist was the greatest. We, who are in Christ, are greater than John the Baptist because **we are born of the Holy Spirit!** We have been given so much more.

Test every spirit by applying the Word of the Lord to what you see. Also apply the Word of the Lord to what you hear. Even the Lord said, "By this you will know what I have spoken, if the word comes to pass." If the Lord said it, it must surely come to pass. If it is from the devil, it will not come to pass--unless a Christian helps him by continuing to share the evil vision or dream with others.

When someone brings a vision or dream to you and you discern it is not from the Lord, do not agree with the person. In a nice way, stop the person and tell him or her to cancel the vision or dream. Show the person, by the Word of the Lord, the scriptures that were violated by the vision or dream. Let the person see the scriptures for himself or herself.

Note: Teacher, instruct the students that God can show you a vision or a dream of the devil's plan against you. Usually, He will begin to prompt you to pray. Or, you would wake up knowing that you have not seen a good plan and you will begin to pray. In God's visions and dreams, evil is not portrayed as good or noble.

You must always ask the Lord for the meaning of your visions and dreams, even if you think you know what they mean. On numerous occasions, the Lord has given me a different interpretation of a vision or a dream about which I thought I knew the meaning.

Example:

Not long after my salvation experience, God the Father informed me that my spirit had asked Him to keep me as the apple of His eye. In response to this request by my spirit, God the Father began to show me visions (the same vision repeated over and over) in which I would see Him sitting on His throne reading a book while I played at His feet. I would see Him turn the pages of the book as He finished each one. Sometimes, He would look away from the book and observe me as I played around his feet like a little child. Just like any father who derives joy from watching his child at play, He would begin to smile as He watched me.

On one occasion, I got a very close look at the book that I always saw Him read. To my amazement, it was blank! I could not understand why God would read a book that was blank and it never occurred to me to ask Him about it. Almost nine years later, when I began to write my first book, He said to me, *"You thought that I was reading a book every time you saw the blank book in my hand. What you did not know was that I was writing a book! You are the blank pages of my book that I am writing. The book is about your life."*

Prior to His words, I was so sure that I had seen Him reading a book each time in the visions. The Word of God gives us clarity concerning visions and dreams and in life as a whole.

End Teaching Here

Activation

This is the part of the class where you gather the students together and:
- You identify new members in the class who are Spirit-filled and would like to receive the Anointing of skills in visions and dreams.
- You lay hands on them to receive the anointing.
- You pray for the entire class.

Session on Actual Dreams and Their Interpretations

This is the part of the class where class members share their dreams and everyone believes the Lord for understanding of the dreams.

Note:
- All interpretations must be based on scriptures.
- Everyone in the class should be allowed to participate, even if their answers are wrong.

- Listen carefully to identify any error in each answer as the students speak **(use the blank notes at the end of each lesson to record each student's interpretation.)**
- Allow everyone to give his or her interpretation before you address each response.
- Identify all inaccurate interpretations and address them.
- Summarize the accurate points that were identified by the students and address any portion of the dream still needing interpretation.

Note:

Most students will skip portions of the dream that they do not understand, so be sure to address those portions of the dream.

Below is an actual dream. Examine the different interpretations and see what other revelations you and the students receive concerning it.

A Friend's Missing Purse Dream

I had forgotten my purse. It was put up in a cabinet or something like a cabinet. There were a lot of people around and we were in a warehouse-like building. We were going out and I turned back to go get my purse. I went into a door way and under my feet was a four- foot wide and four- inches thick concrete with no stairs. It had a huge machine blocking my way. As and I tried to squeeze through, then the machine fell off the block. A man tried to catch it and he too fell and his body tumbled in the air. Then I started to panic but I told myself, "Please Lord, do not let me panic but let me get some help." Then I started to tell two women. Then, I woke up.

Interpretations

Note: Mary's comments are **in boldface**. The *italicized words* are the student's words that Mary addressed.

Misa's Interpretation

The purse represents your friend's finances. There are some apparent hindrances and blockages. Ask the Lord to reveal where you have been neglectful in that area and ask Him for wisdom in how you handle your money.

Instructor: Misa, I think your interpretation of the above dream is right on. Look again at the nature of the blockages. They are designed to keep her from getting to her purse and from getting help when the machine fell off. Even the person that wanted to help her was hindered, also.

Janis's Interpretation

Her prosperity is waiting for her to claim. She almost walked away from it, but then, when she went back to claim it, she encountered obstacles and dead-ends which started to make her panic. She pressed through and the Lord even destroyed her enemies. She called on the Lord, and He sent her two angels/intercessors.

I believe that this is a symbolic dream of instruction from the Lord given to encourage her, and to forewarn of what she will encounter, or explain what she is presently encountering.

Instructor: Janis, that was a good attempt. Yes, she almost walked away from her valuable and her prosperity (purse). But, she thought she had it safely put away in a cabinet and now she cannot get to it. You are right about the obstacles, but they were not destroyed in the dream. The only good thing in the dream is that she called on the name of the Lord. We do not know from the dream that the two women were angels or intercessors. Nothing was resolved in this dream.

Anita's Interpretation

In this dream, the enemy is boasting of what he wants to try to do in your finances by stealing and blocking. Cancel his assignment against you. Do not let fear come in for God has not given you a spirit of fear. He has given you the Spirit of power, love and a sound mind.

Instructor: That was very good, Anita. You nailed the enemy in this dream and you exposed him. I am very impressed. Keep it up. You did not address her calling on the Lord and the two women.

Robin's Interpretation

This is not a dream from God, but from the adversary. He is boasting about his tactics to steal, kill, and destroy. Your purse represents finances that he has devised to block and cause difficulty to retrieve. If you attempt to retrieve what rightfully belongs to you, he will use large barriers to bring disaster upon those who attempt to help you in anyway.

Don't allow the adversary to intimidate you with fear, lies, loss, and destruction. According to John 8:44, Satan is the father of lies and no truth is found in him. Cancel all the lies the enemy has tried to boast about concerning your finances. Do this by speaking the promises of God's Word of prosperity over your life. I would suggest you not repeat this dream to others about the enemy's tactics. **Instructor: Robin, you got it. You exposed the enemy's intention and, again, you comforted the dreamer. This is very good.**

Note to class members: The dreamer sent "The Missing Purse Dream" to me via e-mail before it was shared with the Visions and Dreams Class for interpretation. Here is my interpretation of the dream that I sent her in reply.

Hi ...,

This is Mary. I got your dream and I wanted to encourage you by telling you that it is just the devil trying to play on your intelligence.

First, about your purse--the devil is trying to tell you that you will suffer loss in that area and that he can even block your way as you try to retrieve your finances (purse). The falling machine and the falling man are just extra blockages to keep you from getting help as you attempt to retrieve your purse. The good news is that the devil is a liar and he boasts of things that he cannot do. You do not have to receive his dream or agree with him. Just cancel the dream and speak God's abundance and protection over your finances.

Do not pay the devil any mind.

Mary

Teacher's Notes and Students' Comments

Teacher's Notes and Students' Comments

Teacher's Notes and Students' Comments

Teacher's Notes and Students' Comments

Conclusion

After reading this manual, those who want to develop and master the skills of operating in the gift of interpreting visions and dreams will have a good understanding of why God uses visions and dreams. They will be well-equipped to instruct others on:

- The key principles in visions and dreams
- The sources of visions and dreams
- How to identify the sources of visions and dreams
- How to analyze the contents of visions and dreams
- The different types of visions and dreams

This manual is designed to help pastors teach the basic principles of understanding and interpreting visions and dreams.

It will help book club members, Bible study groups and anyone with the gift of seeing to properly instruct others on visions and dreams.

It is a teacher's aid that will facilitate classroom discussions and dialogues to help students or church members understand more accurately how, and why, God uses visions and dreams.

Because Christians and non-Christians dream, this manual is designed to help anyone desiring knowledge about visions and dreams. However, since it is the Holy Spirit that actually interprets visions and dreams, an individual would need to have a personal revelation of the saving grace of the Lord Jesus Christ before he or she could operate the gift of interpreting visions and dreams God's way, or understand visions and dreams more accurately.

Students' Testimonials

The following are testimonials from some of the students who attended the Visions and Dreams classes.

Rupert G. and Leila May Williams

It has been a great pleasure and a privilege for Leila and me to be able to participate in the teaching of visions and dreams. We have learned that the outpouring of the Holy Spirit through visions and dreams can be a significant part of one's life. We must realize that Mary Ogenaarekhua has been given a God-blessed gift and authority to teach the interpretation of visions and dreams. I thank God for giving her this spiritual ability and for enabling her to take His message visions and dreams to His chosen people—the church!

-Rupert G. Williams

Eva Hizown

Opportunity to participate in the visions and dreams class is an exciting adventure for me.
I never thought that it is possible to see God's direction, warning and encouragement through
dreams. Since I came to America, God has communicated with me intensively through
dreams. Dreams are mysteries that have to be revealed. Jesus taught the people with parables,
which He later explained only to His disciples. In the same way, dreams are one of the languages
that God uses to lead His people. They have to be explained in order to get full understanding and
insight.

I thank God that the gift of interpreting dreams is starting to develop in the body of Christ. I see it
as a powerful and mighty weapon in the kingdom of God and a dangerous threat to the kingdom
of darkness.

-Eva

Robin S. Bright

Since the inception of the Vision and Dreams class in September 2003, my understanding of God's word has especially increased in the area of the prophetic. The teachings provided in these training sessions by Mary Ogenaarekhua have made me aware that God desires to speak directly to me and through me using pictures and images. Gaining an understanding of this was a tremendous contribution in helping me to maneuver through the prophetic realm. Having no prior understanding or experience of how God functions in the area of visions and dreams, Mary's teachings were the steppingstones that helped dispel my ignorance in those areas.

 I thank GOD for using Mary Ogenaarekhua's personal experiences to bring these teachings to the body of Christ for such a time as this.

Ecclesiastes 3:1
"To every thing there is a season, and a time to every purpose under the heaven"

-Robin S. Bright

Margaret Smith

In the dream class, I learned to discern whether my dreams were from God or from the enemy. A powerful tool we learned was to reject the dreams that are not from God and to send them back to where they came from. This has helped bring me great peace and comfort and showed me how to exercise my authority and victory in Christ.

-Margaret Smith

David and Joyce Smith

We have been blessed to know and learn from the ministry gift known as Mary Ogenaarekhua. "Mary O." flows in her God-given Anointing and is eager to share with others. Secure Foundation Bible Church, where we pastor, declares that its mission is to:
- Inform
- Activate
- Empower

Mary Ogenaarekhua does exactly that by removing the veil of misinformation and secrecy. She informs us through the Word of God, Activates us through the workshop application and Empowers us through the impartation of the Anointing of the Holy Ghost. We encourage pastors and leaders to avail themselves of this wonderful opportunity.

-Pastors David and Joyce Smith

Crystal Alman

For the last four years, in the midst of major upheaval in my personal life as well as in my fashion textile company, I began to have dreams, which I felt were from God, warning me of things to come. Many of them froze me with panic, causing me to cry out to God for protection. When I began training with the "Dream Team," I began to learn how to interpret according to the Spirit's mind (Word of God) as well as how to cut off the enemy's lies and deceptions. The main thing that I have learned is that dreams have to line up with the Word of God—that has brought me safety from the enemy's confusion! That helps me to face the storm and go through it with God's authority to win the battle I'm in.

-Crystal

Susan A. Smith

I joined the Dream Team in May 2004 and have been tremendously blessed in a short period of time. The environment is certainly conducive for the move of the Holy Spirit. Ms. Ogenaarekhua's biblical teachings are precept upon precept and line upon line. I have gained a greater appreciation for the outpouring of the Holy Spirit through dreams and visions.

Dreams have been a significant part of my life since childhood. This class affords me the opportunity to build upon the foundation that has already been laid. I realize more than ever that I must discern the source of my dreams. The power lies within me to spoil the plans of the enemy through prayer. I will exercise this God-given authority so that the dream of the enemy will not bring forth fruit. Importantly, I must be careful to appropriate God's promises.

I am thankful and do not take lightly what is being provided for me through this class. I count it a privilege and an honor to understand the Lord's ways at a deeper level. Ms. Ogenaarekhua continues to stress the value of testing the spirit by the Word of God. The Word of God is the tool that we must use to interpret these dreams and visions. There must be awareness that the Holy Spirit is the actual interpreter. My desire is to continue to flow in the interpretation of dreams and visions.
TO GOD BE THE GLORY,

-Susan A. Smith

Kristina Brown

The "Dream Class" was a great experience for me. I got answers that I was looking for and useful knowledge about what I was not familiar with. It also gave me answers and explanation of the troubling dreams that I had and it took away my fears.

I learned more about God and His will. I also learned how to protect myself and how to fight with the kingdom of darkness.

With great appreciation.

-Kristina Brown

Janis E. Yates

From the moment that I first came to the Dreams and Visions class, I was challenged and lifted to a higher level of thinking. The first dream of mine that was interpreted by the class helped me understand some basic guidelines of which I was unaware.

I often like very simple teachings that have profound and lasting impact because they are easy to remember, easy to apply, and easy to teach. Finding out that I could simply cancel a dream is one of those nuggets that can liberate anyone from torment and misdirection. Imagine, something as simple as canceling the dream! The enemy has designed many subtle ways to keep us in ignorance. we know that he is a liar and that he is already defeated! This class has certainly solidified that, from the smallest areas in our life to the largest, knowledge is power and understanding is key.

I am in awe of God and how He has planted such a rich application of scripture in Mary, as it pertains to dreams and visions. This opportunity has also awakened new thinking and discernment about the spirit realm. I am still astounded by some of the personal encounters with demons which Mary shares. I am always blessed. After each class, I always spend my drive home in conversation with the Holy Spirit about whatever He had imparted to me that particular night.

Even more personally, her level of understanding has allowed me to receive a deeper understanding of what the Spirit has deposited in me. This is definitely a time in my life when I am walking into a fuller understanding of who I have been created to be. This class, and more specifically the Anointing upon Mary, have advanced my understanding and development.

-Janis

Pat Felty

The dream and visions class has taught me how to identify whether my dream is from God, the devil or myself. It has helped me to understand that God can send us dreams to warn us about what the devil is planning to do so that we can cancel the devil's plan. I once had a dream in which the devil tried to kill my daughter in a car accident but I prayed when I woke up. My daughter truly did have a car accident shortly after but she survived because I prayed. According to her, something (supernatural) turned the steering wheel away from hitting a pole when her car hydroplaned!

Prior to attending the visions and dreams class, I was not aware that you could cancel a bad dream. I will definitely continue to attend the visions and dreams class because there is a lot I need to know.

-Pat

Anita Williams

Mary, I have been so blessed by the dream and vision teachings. It is such good and sound teaching that lines up with the Word of God.

As we began learning, many opportunities to operate in this anointing became open. I, along with the other believers, received being activated and charged to flow. By listening to the Holy Spirit speak wisdom, we were able to impart revelation to things that seemed to be unknown. This has truly been a reminder and a confirmation that what God did in the days of old, He is still doing today; dreams and visions have not died out!! I've learned even how to come against what the enemy wants to boast about doing and cancel his plans.

I highly recommend and encourage people to read the book and apply the teaching. God has so anointed Mary to interpret and activate. She is a Reproducer of Producers for the Kingdom. There is an overflowing river inside this vessel that the Father wants us to drink from--a river of living water that will satisfy any that thirst for the things of God.

-Anita

Tammy Caston

Before entering the dream interpretation classes, I did not understand the power of godly and ungodly dreams. Nor did I understand God's divine principles of my dreams. I learned to always write my dreams out to the fullest because God is trying to speak to me through my dreams. Dreams will play an important part in your life because God will also use dreams to minister deliverance to you. Know that your spirit never sleeps. A dream is a series of thoughts, images or emotions occurring during sleep. A dream can bring direction and convey the mind of God.

What you fear might surface in your dreams. This is because dreams tell us much about our strengths and our weaknesses. Once you conquer fear in your dreams, you have also conquered it in your life. The Holy Spirit will quicken a dream to address a situation. Every detail in a dream is there for a purpose.

I thank God and Mary for the opportunity to gain wisdom and knowledge concerning my dreams.

-Tammy

Janet Odigie

Before I attended the dream and vision class that is conducted by sister Mary Ogenaarekhua,
I knew little about the importance of dreams and visions. In fact, the first day I was in the class,
I learned something I have never heard about before—how to analyze the contents of your visions
and dreams. Since then, I have taken every aspect of my visions and dreams to be very important
and I use the knowledge I gained from her class to interpret them.

Thank you sister Mary for blessing me through the visions and dreams class.

-Janet

Latrese Fowler

I give glory, honor and praise to God the Father, Most High. I praise God that the Dreams and Visions class is such a blessing. It is a release of knowledge, wisdom and revelation on the different types of dreams and the sources of our dreams--God, self and Satan. Thank God also for the love, compassion and revelation of our teacher, who has an intimate relationship with Jesus. Hallelujah.

-Sister Latrese Fowler

Montrea Pope

Greetings in the name of the Lord of Hosts, our powerful King, the Lord God strong and mighty in battle!
I thank God for the opportunity to attend the visions and dreams classes. The power-packed teachings have helped bring clarity and maturity to this often-misunderstood area—visions and dreams. In this area of the prophetic realm, the Holy Spirit leads us, guide, warns, speaks to us and brings revelation.
In this final age that is drenched with snares, occult, demonic warfare and evil schemes, we as the saints must be fully equipped to receive and interpret revelation from the language of God in visions and dreams.

This class has increased my ability to discern communication and warnings from the Most High and the snares of the devil through visions and dreams! I have come to realize that the Word of God is the bottom line when it comes to the interpretation of visions and dreams. God's Word is still the discerner of visions and dreams.

I have also developed understanding in classification of types and sources of visions and dreams. God gave Daniel skills and understanding in the interpretation of visions and dreams and the gift is not limited to the saints of the Old Testament. It is still available to all His children today!

-Montrea

Bibliography

<u>Webster's II New Riverside University Dictionary</u>, Houghton Miffin Company. Adapted and reproduced by permission from *Webster's II New College Dictionary*. Copyrighted 2001, U.S.A.

<u>Unveiling the God-Mother</u>, Ogenaarekhua, Mary. Published by To His Glory Publishing Co. Inc., Atlanta, Georgia, USA 2004, (pp. 63-64).

TO HIS GLORY PUBLISHING COMPANY, INC.

111 Sunnydale Court, Lawrenceville, GA 30044, U. S. A. (770) 458-7947

Order Form for Bookstores

Order Date: _____

Order Placed By: _____

Address: _____

_____

City _____ ST/ZIP _____

Phone#: _____

Email: _____

Purchase Order#: _____

By fax: _____

By phone: _____

Terms: _____

Discount: _____

Return Policy: Within 1 Year but not before 90 days

Title and ISBN#

Price	Quantity	List Price
Shipping Method:		
Media		
UPS		
FedEx		
Other (please describe)	**Total Quantity:**	
Total Price:		

Ship To Address: Bill To Address:

TO HIS GLORY PUBLISHING COMPANY, INC. (770) 458-7947 Use Only - Billing Information

Books by Mary J. Ogenaarekhua

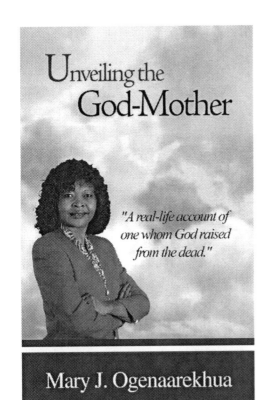

Printed in the United States
67891LVS00001B/53-78

9 780974 980201